The Autism Trail Guide

Postcards from the Road Less Traveled

An anthology of columns, essays and insights

by Ellen Notbohm

Author of *Ten Things Every Child with Autism Wishes You Knew* and *Ten Things Your Student with Autism Wishes You Knew*

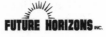

FUTURE HORIZONS INC.
Arlington, TX

THE AUTISM TRAIL GUIDE:
Postcards from the Road Less Traveled

All marketing and publishing rights guaranteed to and reserved by:

Future Horizons, Inc.
721 W. Abram Street
Arlington, TX 76013

(800) 489-0727
(817) 277-0727
(817) 277-2270 Fax

Website: *www.FHautism.com*
E-mail: *info@FHautism.com*

Website: *www.ellennotbohm.com*
E-mail: *emailme@ellennotbohm.com*

ISBN: 1-932565-50-7
ISBN 13: 978-1932565-50-8

Also by Ellen Notbohm

Ten Things Every Child with Autism Wishes You Knew

ForeWord 2005 Book of the Year Honorable Mention
iParenting 2005 Media Award

1001 Great Ideas for Teaching and Raising Children with Autism Spectrum Disorders with co-author Veronica Zysk

Learning *Magazine's 2006 Teachers' Choice Award*

Ten Things Your Student with Autism Wishes You Knew

ForeWord 2006 Book of the Year finalist
iParenting 2006 Media Award

For Connor and Bryce

And for Mark—
their father, my life partner

Acknowledgements

MOST OF THE ESSAYS IN THIS ANTHOLOGY HAVE APPEARED PREVIOUSLY in my columns, my books, or other publications. In some cases, they are expanded from the form in which they originally appeared.

From my column "Postcards from the Road Less Traveled" in *Autism Asperger's Digest*:

"Uncommon Gifts for Uncommon Kids" (2004), "Risk is Not a Four-Letter Word," "The Wind Beneath My Wings," "If You Never Start" (2005), "It Takes a Mantra," "When Math Doesn't Add Up," "Ready for K ... and Beyond," "Pomp and Circumstance," "Solving the Behavior Equation," "Rx for Battle Fatigue" (2006), "Seven Pillars of Wisdom," "What We Leave Unsaid," "A Thing Worth Having", "A Cool Pool Story" (2007)

Bottomless thanks to my editor and muse, Veronica Zysk.

From my column "Exceptional Children: Navigating Special Education and Learning Disabilities," *Children's Voice* (Child Welfare League of America):

"The Other Side of the Desk," "So Many Books, So Little Time," "What Tiggers Do Best" (2007)

Special thanks to Steve Boehm, editor-in-chief (and my favorite Klingon).

Expanded from my column "The Seventh Sense," *Portland Family Magazine*:

"I Sound Like My Mother—I Hope!" (2004), "The Power of a Cookie" (2005), "The Gift of an Experience" (originally "Real Boys Love Ballet") (2005)

One-of-a-kind thanks to Brittney Corrigan-McElroy, not just for contributing her perfect poetry to this book, but for being the one in a million person who could room with a perfect stranger—me—one on one for a whole week and make it a dream experience.

Ongoing appreciation to Wayne Gilpin and Kelly Gilpin at Future Horizons for continuing to let me inflict my voice on the world. And the same only more so to my mother Henny and my late great father David for giving me that voice, and to my husband Mark, who chooses every day to keep listening.

And there will never be words adequate to thank the loves of my life, Connor and Bryce.

But they know.

Two roads diverged in a wood, and I—
I took the one less traveled by,
And that has made all the difference.

– Robert Frost

Table of Contents

Beforeword

By Veronica Zysk

Ellen Notbohm is a clever woman. She's a clever mom to her two boys, Connor (the eldest) and Bryce (now a teen). She's a clever writer, able to turn an interesting phrase whether she's writing about some humdrum topic or one that flames the fires of inner passions—like ancestry ... or autism. She's a clever speaker one-on-one or one-on-hundreds, as well being quite clever in navigating both charted and uncharted waters of her school system, advocating for her children's needs.

Just what do I mean by "clever"? The *American Heritage Dictionary* defines the word as "mentally quick and original; bright." *Roget's 21st Century Thesaurus* offers a long list of applicable synonyms: able, adept, brilliant, discerning, expert, handy, inventive, keen, knowledgeable, nobody's fool, quick-witted, sensible, sharp, skillful, smart, sprightly, versatile, wise.

Yes, Ellen Notbohm is, indeed, a clever person. She is all those things, and more. I know this from a history of experiences she and I have shared—both professional and personal—that cognitively span just a few short earthly years, yet intuitively feel as though they have been going on for lifetimes.

So it comes as no surprise to those of us who know her and have experienced her distinctive blend of curiosity and common sense that *The Autism Trail Guide: Postcards from the Road Less Traveled*, would echo this cleverness both in form and content. (Didn't you wonder why this section is called a Beforeword, rather than a Foreword? Ah, that's a surprise yet to come!) After all, it arrives on the heels of three other award-winning, thought-provoking, mind-expanding books: *1001 Great Ideas for Teaching and Raising Children with Autism Spectrum Disorders,* which Ellen and I co-authored; *Ten Things Every Child with Autism Wishes You Knew,* a dynamite little book that shatters commonplace thought about children on the autism spectrum, and *Ten Things Your Student with Autism Wishes You Knew* (another Ellen-Veronica collaboration).

What is it about this fourth book that captures its five star rating? Simply this: there's something for everyone, from a parent who found everything for someone—her child, her son.

There are no cookbook recipes for what to do for a child with autism spectrum disorders (ASDs). Every child is different. Every child with autism or Asperger's Syndrome will present symptoms and characteristics in a unique manner. Rebecca has sensory issues or behavior problems, but they may be a world apart from those Joshua experiences. It's the consummate Catch-22 of autism that sets this disorder apart from others: *we never know* what the future holds, because autism does not inherently limit their potential.

We who love or care for these individuals can see autism as a burden or we can choose to see that it does not define our children, that our children are, above all else, individuals, and then learn to live with, and even thrive with their autism. It's an important distinction, one that affects attitude. And, as Ellen knows and articulates every chance possible: your attitude will produce the reality of how you view this journey you're on. See it as a prison sentence and that's what you'll experience. See it as a force that offers you room for expansion in yet unimaginable ways, and you will find your life enriched by the experience.

Every single child, teen, and adult with ASD is like a snowflake: a one-of-a-kind marvel of nature never to be repeated again despite the mega-billions of snowflakes that will follow. Ellen *gets* this: truly, madly and deeply.

Beforeword

Right from the start, when Bryce was identified with autism at age three, she saw him first as a child. Yes, a child with autism but a child first and foremost. She understood in body, mind and spirit, and believed to depths that reached down to her cellular levels, that there was no limit to his potential. *This she believed.* From that point forward, with the unwavering conviction that only a mother-on-a-mission possesses, she paved the road less traveled carefully enough that at every step, every turn, at every fork in the road, Bryce had a well-marked trail to follow no matter where he found himself.

This book offers you the trail markers to do the same for your child.

A myriad of options exist today for helping our children and adults with ASD. How are parents to make informed choices for their children? There are no easy answers, no special made-just-for-you concoction of products or therapies that deliver an abracadabra magical reversal of autism. Parents search for that wizardry and frantically hope for that cure. To date, it hasn't materialized. What does appear, to our great fortune, are parents like Ellen, who have pioneered the vast landscape of autism and come forward to help, to be your Autism Trail Guide.

So, just as Ellen the author has cleverly assembled a collection of writings that is, in and of itself, a trail guide, Ellen the parent comes to you as your personal trail guide, sharing a mother's own hard-won wisdom to steer you on your sojourn.

Her essays will amuse you, enlighten you, and educate you about life when autism is part of the mix. Take her lessons and let them become torch lights, illuminating your path. And like any expert trail guide who finds a place in your heart, Ellen offers her inimitable brand of real-life wisdom with humor, wit and yes, a special dose of cleverness that is uniquely Ellen Notbohm. Hers is one travel experience you'll remember and return to again and again as you tread your own road less traveled.

Veronica

May 2007

Veronica Zysk is a previous Executive Director of the Autism Society of America, an author and editor in the autism community, and Managing Editor of the *Autism Asperger's Digest*, a bimonthly national magazine devoted to autism spectrum disorders. She and Ellen first met when Ellen submitted an article to the *Digest*, and was subsequently invited to pen a regular parent-to-parent column, "Postcards from the Road Less Traveled." Their personal and professional collaboration expanded into writing what has become a series of award-winning books. Veronica and Ellen both agree: their partnership holds the promise of unlimited adventure in coming years. The drawing board is knee-deep in ideas. Which road-less-traveled will call them next?

Preface

"START AT THE BEGINNING," THE MAD HATTER TELLS ALICE IN Wonderland. "And when you get to the end—stop."

I never cared much for *Alice in Wonderland*, and now I wonder if it's because a purely linear story with a clear beginning, middle and end is just too much fantasy for me! If there is one thing of which the journey through autism has convinced me, it is that life and all our relationships within it is composed of circles, not straight lines, and the richness and the essence of being alive derives from those circles and their infinite number of places to begin.

I began writing my "Postcards from the Road Less Traveled" column in 2004, and the point in time I chose to begin was a moment during my son Bryce's first grade year. The school, Capitol Hill Elementary, had a wonderful program called All-Stars. Each month, several students from each class would be featured in a school-wide assembly. The teachers would introduce each student, note a few things that made each individual special, and then each student would answer a question. The question was the same for all students throughout the year. Over the course of the year, every student would be an All-Star.

Bryce was a first-grader in 1999. Buzz about the new millennium, Y2K, was pervasive. The question of the year for the All-Stars was: what would you like to be in the new millennium? On a crisp late winter day, I watched a string of charming first graders step up to the stage to answer the question. A soccer star! is the most popular response. One after another, they want to be pop singers, race car drivers, cartoon artists, millionaires, veterinarians, and firefighters.

Bryce, in his first-ever encounter with a microphone, answered simply: "I think I'd just like to be a grown-up."

Applause broke out and the principal announced: "The world would be a better place if more people aspired to what Bryce aspires to."

Scene-skip across four years and suddenly Bryce is in fifth grade, and this will be his last All-Star assembly. For every year previous, my husband, my mother and I have all attended All-Stars together, but this year, travel and work schedules have collided and I will be attending alone.

The question for the students this year is: describe yourself as a dictionary entry with at least three definitions. Most of the kids start with: I'm a noun. A couple are verbs. Then the definitions begin: 1. a soccer player (of course); 2. good at math, 3. love to tease my sister. Or: 1. A Nintendo champ; 2. great at drawing; 3. eat ice cream every day. One girl makes everyone sit up straight by saying, I like to help others.

Bryce steps to the microphone, and with complete aplomb, reads from his card:

"Bryce. (brīs) Noun. 1. a student who always tries my best. 2. a writer in my spare time, and 3. –

"Someone who loves my parents."

An audible intake of breath sweeps the auditorium and everyone who knows me swivels around to see if I am going to burst into tears.

I would, except that all the muscles in my face are suddenly paralyzed. Bryce is, as usual, unaware of the fact that he has done something extraordinary; he throws his serene smile my way, with a thumbs-up and a look of "there, I did it." He found me in the crowd a few minutes later when the assembly broke up, handed me his All-Star award, which carried not only his definition of himself but a photo taken in front of a towering camellia bush on the school grounds. I can't help thinking, admiring the photo, that the camellia isn't the only thing in the photo that is in full bloom.

I did make it to the car that day before letting loose and sobbing into the cell phone to my husband, *you picked the wrong one to miss!*

I thought back over all the years I had spent yearning for and wondering if my very language-challenged child would ever say "I love you, Mommy." I never prompted him to do so because I wanted it to come from within him, or not at all. I never, ever could have dreamed that when that time came, it would be in front of a microphone, to the whole world.

I believe my wish to hear those words is nearly universal among autism moms (and dads too). I won't say "be careful what you wish for or you might get it." I will say only to be aware that one fine day your most fervent wish may just walk right up and bite you on the nose when you least expect it.

It's what makes getting out of bed every morning so worth it.

It took me some years to realize that what Bryce wrote in his dictionary definition of himself was also a perfect description of me. This poses a question that I can't answer for you: chicken or egg? A great reflective light is at work here, but the source of the light (Is he reflecting me or am I reflecting him?) is unclear. I love that. This circular, reflective energy is what leap-frogs us down our road less traveled.

Being chosen for the privilege of parenting Bryce and Connor was surely the highest honor I'll receive in this lifetime, but not far behind was the privilege of being asked to write my column "Postcards from the Road Less Traveled" for *Autism Asperger's*

Digest. I think of myself as "just a mom" like so many others, but editor Veronica Zysk thought there was more. "Ellen is," Veronica told *Digest* readers, "a real-world parent of a child with autism, on a real-world journey, open eyes, open heart, willing to take a stand when need be and knowing when to walk away and fight another day. I have no doubt that you will be enriched beyond measure by the thoughts, feelings and advice of this practical lady, a sparkling woman of substance." Well, that described a pretty extravagant mission, one in which I didn't dare let her down.

I didn't know it then, but I began writing this book on the same day I began writing the "Postcards" column. Through the years, I sculpted and Veronica finessed my experiences into words that reached and touched many *Digest* readers, and they wrote to tell me so. I began to feel that these columns, wrought so lovingly and sometimes so painfully, deserved to be shared with a wider audience. This book allows that to happen.

I think of the essays in this book as trips to the toolshed wherein we store all the virtual hardware needed for this creative construction project that is our child with autism. As autism is a shifty foe, so shift our needs, seemingly with the wind, from day to day and even from hour to hour. Sometimes we need a machete to hack through the education bureaucracy. Sometimes we need insect repellant to deal with the inevitable unkindness of strangers. Sometimes we need a cultivator to sow and encourage the growth we know will come if we are patient and steadfast in our work. And sometimes we need a soldering iron to weld our broken hearts back together. All of this you will find in these pages as we tackle a spectrum of challenges from nuts-and-bolts everyday issues such as math homework, video games, and tricky behavior to the larger life issues that have no simple answers. When to take risks and when to play it safe. When to step up and when to back off. How to hang on and when to let go.

Some of the thoughts and essays in this anthology do not qualify as autism-specific. I've included them deliberately because it's very important to me that you know that life with a child with autism is not all autism, all the time. Your child is different, yes, but he is also like typical children in many ways. I love Dr. Jed Baker's characterization of people with autism, "the same as everyone else, only more so."* You cannot raise a child with autism without experiencing some of the universalities of child rearing. Parents are on a developmental journey as well, so I've veered off the "child with autism" focus a few times to take a look at some fits and foibles in my own growth. I hope they bring you a smile because, according to my one of my gurus, Mark Twain, "The human race has one really effective weapon, and that is laughter." Being able to laugh at ourselves and with ourselves is, frankly, essential to our journey.

In the course of our journey, my family and I have been blessed with more heroes than anyone should ever be entitled to, and you will meet many of them in this book. But two rise above, two whose influence so eloquently underwrote my ability to be all that I had to be in the face of my children's challenges. One was the pediatrician who was with me on the day I became a mother. The other was the teacher who helped me step over the threshold into adulthood, a decade before I ever dreamed of becoming a mother. Because their insight, guidance and belief in me shaped my entire adult experience, their stories, "You Know More than You Think You Know" and "The Song that Never Ends," stand apart. I very much hope you will draw on the energy of their wisdom as I still do every day of my life.

Let's get started.

* Jed Baker, Ph.D., Director of the Social Skills Training Project (*www.socialskillstrainingproject.com*).

The Road Begins

You Know More Than You Think You Know

A VERY WISE DOCTOR TOLD ME THIS WHEN I HAD BEEN A MOTHER for less than twenty-four hours. He called it his nickel parenting advice but it is actually million-dollar advice

We chose so well when we chose Dr. Springer, and we chose him from a pool of one. We had a list of pediatricians to interview shortly before Connor was born, and he was our first one. After chatting a few moments, he said, "and now I have to ask you a question. Do either of you smoke in the home?"

"No."

"Good," he said, "because I am not able to accept new patients whose parents smoke in the home. I figure if you are going to disadvantage your child's health so greatly right from the beginning, there won't be much I can do to help."

We're impressed. "So," I continue, "I guess you have to treat the mothers as well as the children; at least that's the cliché I've heard about pediatricians."

"Yes, I've heard that one too," he says. "But I guess I've just got all the good moms in town because it's never been an issue for me."

We didn't interview any more doctors.

From time to time—and not nearly often enough—we would receive in the mail a small treatise from Dr. Springer expounding on some aspect or other of life in general as it would relate to kids. I loved those epistles, but only as Bryce's childhood slowly unfolded in its onion-like layers did I realize how profound and multifarious these apparent stream-of-consciousness musings were.

He wrote about strength:

> Once upon a time little girls were made of sugar and spice and everything nice; little boys were made of snips and snails and puppy dog tails. What exactly is a snip? The children I know are nearly 100% puppy dog tails, both boys and girls. Who needs sugar and spice? It melts in the rain or even if you sweat.
>
> Mother Nature gives us this wonderful start. Why do most people stop running around at age twelve? "I didn't make the team." Before twelve and after twenty nobody has to make the team. Try frisbee or skiing; the rules are more flexible. "I catch balls with my head." Me too, but when you have an hour let me list all the sports that don't use a ball. "I'm too tired." Okay, this is a problem of strength so listen closely.
>
> Strength is acquired, not genetic. It is mental as well as physical. It's easy to recognize people who glow, are able to weather distress with grace and also have high self-esteem. Sounds perfect for all children; sounds perfect for all parents.
>
> The path to strength must be completely non-critical of self, just like the spontaneous play of little kids. Running is the one I know. Start slowly, be completely non-critical and walk more than jog. The body is in charge, not the ego. Three months is plenty soon to be running and then not for the whole hour. It must be playful. The stupidest path to strength is chemical. Steroids never did anything for anyone's mental strength.

> Don't change anything about yourself except the urge to start and keep going. Starting me takes five minutes, my engine is slower than a diesel. The eventual delight of play does come, I promise, and then it's hard to stop. Any kind of play counts as long as you work up a sweat. Let me know of your strength. Complain some, brag a lot. Be the perfect model. Children always catch on.

Was he writing specifically about Bryce or did it just seem that way? Nearly every word was pertinent.

Dr. Springer did not figure largely in the specific approaches taken to Bryce's autism or in the specific treatment of Connor's ADHD; he retired when Bryce was only six. But he's always been a spiritual presence shepherding my work with the children. Though he never gave me direct advice about autism, his low-key common-sense approach to parenting in general became my most valuable tool in dealing with autism.

Connor at five years old was an ADHD sunflower in full bloom. Dr. Springer loved him at face value. "I'm not the one to ask about ADHD. I don't see him in social or educational settings. I see him one-on-one in my office, and he is great. He doesn't climb the blinds and tip over the fish tank. However, if the people who are with him six hours a day are telling you something different, I suggest you listen to them. Then come back to me with all the information, and we'll talk some more.

"In the meantime," he said, with his slowly-spreading smile that told me a zinger was coming, "if you take that kid to a restaurant, you deserve what you get."

It was his gentle way of telling me that we cannot always slot our children conveniently into the activities and the lifestyle we want. Their inability to handle certain experiences and social settings at various developmental stages of their childhood is not a deliberate attempt to sabotage our lives or make us miserable. They are not "out to get us"; they are merely children with very limited life experience. If, like my children, they have the complexities of neuro-pediatric disorders layered on top, it is stunning to think of what they faced in getting through their days. From Dr. Springer, I learned to accept the day-to-day challenges of both autism and ADHD with a certain level of objectivity that allowed me to bypass some of the frustration, exasperation and self-pity. I had a choice: I could look at their limitations as restrictive or oppressive, or I could see them as opportunities. Having to develop a constant stream of Plan Bs is a skill which I am now very grateful to have, even though—or maybe *because*—it was forced upon me. Friends, I am *very* good at it, and it is one of my proudest achievements. I never feel stuck; how great is that?

Those so-called limitations meant that during our children's early years, large family get-togethers were most often at our house since that's what the kids handled best. Family members and friends who cared about our kids and understood their challenges were frequent visitors for what were almost always fun and boisterous happenings. The others—well, we didn't see them very much. It was their choice and their loss.

By late childhood/early adolescence, both kids grew into their social selves and went everywhere with us. It's funny how we can't really remember what we missed while simply letting them unfold in their own good time—if in fact we missed anything that mattered.

"Much stress is self-generated," Dr. Springer wrote in another newsletter. He had just observed an SUV sitting halfway into a crosswalk; driver flicking cigarette ashes out the window with one hand and mashing cell phone to ear with the other. The light turned green, the car practically leaped from the pavement and the race was on! "Sixty-five miles an hour is too slow for many of us. But the minute we save adds up to almost nothing in a 1,440-minute day."

And even though he was a devoted exercise advocate, he painted a wry picture of the dogged athlete strapped to that pulse monitor. "Stop to smell the flowers?" he asked satirically. "No way; a runner shouldn't even be *looking* at the flowers or their pulse may slow out of the training range!"

If we are to help our ASD children ease the rigidity of their thinking, we must be prepared to do so ourselves. Look at some of the dispensable pressures in your life: sports pressure, house-perfect pressure, traffic pressure (you can't change it, but you can make use of the time, perhaps by listening to books on CD). In true child-wise fashion, Dr. Springer's two-year-old granddaughter provided the beginnings of a way out for us. Don't even try to push her, he said. She will answer by asking herself, who are the people I really need to please?

Do I really have to?

"The bad phases will pass," he assured me. "Just remember—so will the good ones." He didn't say this as license to disengage from the process of teaching and guiding our children; it was not a declaration of fatalism. It was a reminder that there is always a Big Picture looming as a backdrop to whatever smaller drama of the moment is unfolding. Complacency is the quicksand on one side of the trail, discouragement on the other. For best results, stay on the path.

But the most important gift Dr. Springer gave me was a handful of words left in my swollen, smarting lap when Connor was less than twenty-four hours old.

"I've just come from the nursery," he said, moving briskly across the faded linoleum of my hospital room, "where your son is performing feats of neurological wonder." I couldn't begin to imagine what this meant and I was still in the sleepless fog of a twenty-two-hour labor anyway. Something about gross motor ability, reflexes, eye movements.

He pulled a chair up to the bed. "Here's my nickel advice about parenting," he said. "There are a hundred ways to do any given thing parents have to do. Only thirty of them will even make sense to you. Only ten of those will be anything you might consider trying. And you might get around to actually trying three of those. If you are lucky, one of them will work."

He stood up. "The most important thing is—trust your instinct. You know more than you think you know."

And it turned out that he was being modest with my initial question about treating the moms as well as the kids. No visit to his office ever ended without Mom being summoned to his office to sit in the orange plastic chair across the desk from him so he could ask, "and how are you doing?" Moms, he said, have to take care of themselves if they are to be able to take proper care of their children. Remember—who has the power here? he asked me on a particularly difficult day. *You* have the power.

Oh no, I most certainly do not, I told him. Not today. They do.

Not true, he said. *You* have the power, and you are doing a great job with it....

Every visit ended with him telling me what a great job I was doing. Even when I didn't believe him, the seeds of empowerment were busting through the sod of my self-doubt. I was never a natural mother. The biological clocked ticked past thirty before I even thought about it, and then only to seriously doubt whether I was up to the job. Several years in the orange chair were having an effect. He was instilling in me the self-confidence I would need to own if I wanted to infuse my children with the same.

Trust your instinct. You know more than you think you know.

Postcards from the Front Lines

We didn't enlist; we were drafted. We met the adversary without the benefit of boot camp. We've been dropped directly on to the front line; it is a perilous place, but also one of bold advantage. On the front lines, we cannot be ambushed. It is where we find the shrewdest strategies and tactics, the most potent tools and weapons. From the front lines, we can look our opponent in the eye and see its weaknesses and vulnerabilities, because they are surely there. And from the front lines we can see something not visible from the shadows—the horizon, in all its limitlessness. *Advance.*

It Takes A Mantra

It now seems like a long time ago in a galaxy far, far away, I was learning how to raise a very young child with autism. He didn't much resemble the happy, confident teenager prowling our house today. He was a basically sweet-tempered child but one with very limited verbal skills. His sensory integration difficulties were as yet not fully identified, so, several times a day, my otherwise sweet, loving son would lapse into baffling episodes of hair-tearing, cat-scratching, furniture-throwing violence. He wore clothes only when socially necessary, preferring to go about his business at home clad only in his birthday suit. Many classroom and playtime activities provoked him into physically backing away with his hands over his ears. He laughed at all the wrong times and he didn't seem to experience pain or cold in a typical way.

It was definitely a two steps forward, one step back process. One bleary day, I confided to a friend how hard it was to keep that one-day-at-a-time theme idling in the brain at all times.

One day at a time? she gasped. Oh, no, no, no. That's much too hard. It's one *moment* at a time.

And you know what? Thousands of one-moments-at-a-time later, we are in a happy place.

My friend did me such an outstanding favor. She made me realize that I needed my own personal words of wisdom to live by, not somebody else's clichés. So I went out and found them.

Here is something maybe we can learn from the jocks: mantras, mottoes and motivational slogans are commonplace in athletics. Knute Rockne's "when the going gets tough, the tough get going." Wayne Gretzky's "100% of the shots you don't take don't go in." Yogi Berra's "it ain't over 'til it's over."

Raising a child with autism is as athletic an endeavor as can be found in any venue. It requires extreme stamina, tenacity, vision, sticking to a training schedule that would drop-kick the average athlete. It requires that banal, gag-me phrase, "mental toughness."

You need a mantra. But not a cliché.

The word *mantra* is a compound Sanskrit word meaning, generally "that which frees the mind." (The root *manas* means "mind"; the root *trai* means "to free or protect.") In its purest Hindu or Buddhist form, a mantra is a set of sounds repeated over and over to focus thought. "Om ..." is the stereotypical mantra many people recognize. The theory behind mantras is that when we create vocal sound, it produces vibration. As the sound is repeated over and over, it creates energy. With continued repetition, this energy grows ever stronger and overrides lesser energies. Thomas Ashley-Farrand, author of Healing Mantras, offers a beautifully succinct summary of why we should all have a mantra: "They are formidable. They are ancient. They work."

Mantras don't have to be mystical, antediluvian chantings. They can be crisp and contemporary. And, much like love, you may not find one if you go looking for it. But if you are open to the idea, the right one may find you when you are least expecting it. Mine found me quite unexpectedly in an undistinguished beach-town gift shop. Seaweed-smelling sand grumbled underfoot on the battered plank floor. At eye level were the usual row upon row of shell animals with googly eyes, kites, sand toys, snow globes and T-shirts. I had to look up to see the display of framed aphorisms. There it was, a simple hand-lettered plaque that read:

Courage doesn't always roar.
Sometimes courage is the little voice at the end of the day that says "I will try again tomorrow."

– Mary Anne Radmacher-Hershey © 1994

That puppy came home with me and took up residence on the living room wall over the piano. Many, many were the days that came to an end with me standing in front of it in tears. But I always did get up to try again tomorrow. Over time, imperceptibly, I needed it less and less. Today, I cannot remember the last time I looked at it. Like a true mantra, the energy it generated overpowered the weaker forces of doubt, exhaustion and despondency.

My other favorite mantra is the "Desiderata" by Max Ehrmann. Those of my generation may consider this poem hackneyed thanks to a 1971 pop recording of it by Les Crane.

At that time and since, a lot of silly talk has swirled around about the poem having been found in an old church 300 years ago. But in fact it was written in the early 1900s by Mr. Ehrmann, a Terre Haute, Indiana attorney (1872-1945). "Desiderata" is a Latin plural noun meaning "things that are highly desirable."

Here's the odd thing. I had known the "Desiderata" since I was a teen, even vaguely recall having a poster of it on my wall. As an adult, it was one of those okay, lukewarm memories from more adolescent times. Until, as the mother of Bryce, I came across a particular version of it in a used book store. It was a small, thin book, just 6" x 8" and forty-six pages. It was the layout that enchanted me. Just two lines of the poem appeared in italic type across the bottom of each two-page spread. Each right hand page contained a simple line drawing, in blue. Each left hand page was blank.

In this presentation, the "Desiderata" became no longer just an okay poem. Each line stood by itself, visually underscored ever so subtly by the unpretentious illustrations. The depth of the piece emerged in a way I had never seen before.

As a young child, Bryce had vigorously resisted my efforts to read to him. Of course, I had presented all the usual children's literature. Bafflingly, all had been firmly rejected.

With this "Desiderata," I began to understand how autism had affected Bryce's ability to enjoy books and take in their meaning. When row after row of typeface competes with the color, shape and texture of a typical child's picture book, the input had become overwhelming to him. I marveled at how this simple book, with but a few words on each blessedly uncluttered page, was able to bring its message home so effortlessly.

If you compare yourself with others, you may become vain or bitter, for always there will be greater and lesser persons than yourself.

This became a mini-mantra of mine and it saved me from a lot of anguish I might have experienced comparing Bryce's developmental progress to the typical timeline. I trained myself to measure and compare his progress only against himself: Last year he could not do multiplication and division; this year, he can. Tell time, ride a bike, handle money, swim, read. He did all these things rather like a deliberate echo behind that typical timetable, one to two years later. And the minute he did, we instantly forgot that he ever hadn't, because it simply no longer mattered. After a while, we were able to trust the larger picture, that he eventually would reach many typical benchmarks and milestones, in his own good time. Each time it happened, our anxiety level plummeted.

Sparing ourselves the comparison to others was one of the greatest life lessons Bryce taught us. He always had an innate serenity, even when he began to emerge from the shell of autism, that somehow allowed him to forego judgments against himself. He was (and is) an actual embodiment of the "Desiderata"; he is comfortable with solitude, is gentle with himself, avoids creeps and jerks, is sincere in his affections, very much enjoys his academic and artistic endeavors, strives to be happy. Because of his example, I feel I can do no less.

But do not distress yourself with dark imaginings.
Many fears are born of fatigue and loneliness

If you are reading this as the parent of a child with autism, I know that I am preaching to the choir when I say that it is a job fraught with periods of paralyzing fatigue and loneliness. Even in the best of situations there are times when our spouses, our parents and family members, our school staff or even health professionals simply do not understand or support whatever large or small issue we are grappling with at the moment. Those are the moments when it is most important to hold tight to the facts of our circumstances and not allow misgivings and misapprehension to add false embellishments.

With all its sham, drudgery, and broken dreams,
it is still a beautiful world.

I still choke up over this one on a regular basis. It is perhaps the most important big-picture perspective of all. When Connor was seven, we discovered that we were lucky enough to live in the vicinity of The Children's Program, a diagnostic and treatment facility whose staff included a psychologist who specialized in ADHD. Dr. Jeff Sosne was a Princeton- and Rutgers-trained psychologist whose interest and expertise stemmed from experience with his own son with ADHD. Jeff had developed a very effective ten-week group therapy program for children with ADHD. We completed the ten weeks; it was extremely helpful. I always felt that it had perhaps trained me more than Connor, but no matter, because the end result was the same. Jeff became a sort of ADHD True North to whom we could boomerang back from time to time to get advice, re-acclimate to our goals as Connor grew older and moved up the developmental spectrum from elementary to middle school. That move to middle school was an academic snap for Connor but the social picture was much more complex. As I did every few years, I made an appointment for a touch-base with Jeff. As usual, he was able to provide a short laundry list of actionable suggestions. I thanked him sincerely, with the rueful tag line that "it's an ugly world out there."

He jumped all over that. "No, it is *not* an ugly world." He was emphatic. "You are *not* allowed to teach your children that. It is a *beautiful* world with some ugly things in it."

It was a huge distinction. I do try never to be without it.

Contemporary mantras are to be found all around us, but when the right one finds us, it provides more than just the drumbeat of repetitious words. It provides the steadying hand under your elbow as you walk your path, not leading the way, but lending just enough support to let know you know that you won't lose your balance.

Desiderata

by Max Ehrmann

© 1927, Robert L. Bell

Go placidly amid the noise and the haste,
and remember what peace there may be in silence.

As far as possible without surrender, be on good terms with
all persons.

Speak your truth quietly and clearly, and listen to others,
even to the dull and the ignorant; they too have their story.

Avoid loud and aggressive persons; they are vexatious to the spirit.

If you compare yourself with others, you may become vain or bitter,
for always there will be greater and lesser persons than yourself.

Enjoy your achievements as well as your plans.

Keep interested in your own career, however humble;
it is a real possession in the changing fortunes of time.

Exercise caution in your business affairs, for the world is full of trickery.

But let this not blind you to what virtue there is;
many persons strive for high ideals, and everywhere life
is full of heroism.

Be yourself. Especially do not feign affection.

Neither be cynical about love, for in the face of all aridity
and disenchantment, it is as perennial as the grass.

Take kindly the counsel of the years, gracefully surrendering
the things of youth.

Nurture strength of spirit to shield you in sudden misfortune.

But do not distress yourself with dark imaginings.
Many fears are born of fatigue and loneliness.

Beyond a wholesome discipline, be gentle with yourself.

You are a child of the universe.
No less than the trees and the stars, you have a right to be here.

And whether or not it is clear to you,
no doubt the universe is unfolding, as it should.

Therefore be at peace with God, whatever you conceive Him to be.

And whatever your labors and aspirations in the noisy confusion of life, keep peace in your soul.

With all its sham, drudgery, and broken dreams,
it is still a beautiful world.

Be cheerful. Strive to be happy.

Risk is Not a Four-Letter Word

"It doesn't matter whether they are on the severe end of autism or on the mild end," Bryce's PE teacher told me. "Every child with autism I've ever worked with has an innate feeling of whether or not an adult believes that they 'can do it' or not. When a parent or teacher, knowingly or unknowingly, exhibits a lack of faith in the child—consciously or subconsciously doesn't believe that this child can progress as other children will—the result is a child who shuts off. They catch the lack of belief. They think, 'So why try? Why try if you don't think that I can do it?'"

Children with autism are not the only ones who fall into the why-try? trap. It is present all around in all manner of children and adults. With maturity, some individuals develop a kind of competitive streak that thrives on nay-saying (or nay-thinking). A you-can't-do-it comment becomes a dare and a spur to action. But for many, it's a blockade. Think about your own life experiences. Didn't go out for the tennis team because you didn't think you'd make it? Didn't enter the spelling bee for fear of missing a word and embarrassing yourself? Would like to run for school board but not sure you're smart enough? Didn't go to college because your parents convinced you that getting a job was more important? Fear of failure is surely one of the biggest de-motivators around. The distance between why-try? and can-do is vast but navigable. It requires courage, and courage comes from being comfortable with risk.

In the late 1980s, the Canadian-owned company for which I worked was bought by a large Texas corporation. The new owners sent a variety of corporate officers around to interview key people in the newly acquired subsidiary. One gentleman who came to visit me identified himself as the Vice President of Risk Management. I had never heard this term, but it sounded very safety-on-the-job oriented; I couldn't imagine how it related to my largely desk-bound corporate management duties. After listening to him for a while, I finally got it. "Oh," I said. "You're an insurance guy." Yes, came the reply.

It sounded like doublespeak at first, but I have come to see the value in drawing a parallel between insurance and risk. I expended heroic effort during Bryce's childhood manipulating events and environments to ensure that his life was composed of bite-sized experiences that would build a foundation of success. Some might call that low-risk, but I preferred to phrase it in the positive, calling it confidence-enhancing. I didn't consider it overprotective and I would do it the same way again. I felt it was of paramount importance in the long run to early on create a core of self-esteem and a positive self-image that would, with maturity, fuel him through being able to handle failure.

In early childhood, Bryce had a distressing habit of going into full-strength meltdown at the word "no" or any similar negative verbal feedback. It did not matter how unrealistic the request—he wanted to go to summer camp in December and have Christmas come in July (I guess we could have moved to Australia)—the negative response triggered Armageddon. His attacks on me sometimes drew blood and there are a few walls and doors in our home that still bear telltale dents from hurled furniture and toys. It clearly wasn't the time to teach risk. But bit by bit, it did come. At age seven, he finally released his barnacle grip on the side of the pool and learned to swim. A few weeks later he jumped off the high dive. (It nearly killed me. I could have made the dive from bleachers to pool in one Elastigirl leap.) He went on to compete on the swim team. At ten, the kid who had stood mute in the back row of the kindergarten music program was singing solo on stage as Grandpa Joe in *Charlie and the Chocolate Factory:*

I never thought my life could be anything but catastrophe
But suddenly I begin to see a bit of good luck for me.
I've got a golden ticket!

By age twelve, he had river-rafted, trail-biked, given speeches in front of groups, backpacked, gone crab fishing, thrown shot put and discus on the school track team, asked a girl to the movies, and whooped it up at the school dances.

He succeeded at all these things in part because we had a very flexible and incremental definition of the word "success." It also came because over time, he was able to shake just enough of his literal, black-and-white thinking to begin to understand that risks and consequences are matters of degree. To many children with autism, all risks and all mistakes and all failures and shortcomings are the same size—huge!! Easy to see how paralyzing this can be. Our kids need to be taught (and taught and taught) that no one is perfect (now there's an absolute they should be able to relate to!) and that every so-called failure comes in many degrees. "Failure" does not automatically equate to "disaster." Some failures are merely passing disappointments. Our psychologist espouses the philosophy of No Big Deal. You reduce the intensity of the child's angst by demonstrating (repeatedly) that when the foible is small, it is No Big Deal, whether in terms of effort, time, cost or "fairness." Attitude is contagious, Mom and Dad. Be No Big Deal role models.

So, while children with ASD can be very rigid in their routines and resistant to moving beyond their very narrow comfort zones, it's neither too early nor too late to instill the mantra that everyone makes mistakes. (Connor, now in college, reminds us: "That's what Big Bird says, so it must be true!"). Your child may be more willing to attempt a new challenge if you provide him with a sturdy "risk management" package, insurance that mitigates the fear of failure:

Always acknowledge that the courage is in the effort, not the result.

Maturity and character grow and develop during the process, not at the outcome. It does not matter that the first note he writes you isn't legible. It is a Declaration of Independence! Applaud it as such.

Let him see you trying new things.

One summer on our raft trip, I "shot the swimmer's rapids," which involved riding a short stretch of white water without the boat. Frankly, it was a bit beyond my risk-comfort zone. But I watched dozens of people go before me, many of them older and in much worse physical condition than me. Not one of them slipped by the rescue ropes and they all seemed to love it. Just this once, I told myself, don't be a wiener. After I did it I was proud of myself—and Bryce was visibly impressed, even willing to try it himself (I didn't let him—he wasn't quite a strong enough swimmer yet.). This example may be a tad extreme but you can think of something in your context. And if you can't, how come you aren't trying new things? Learn to knit, build a birdhouse. See a Shakespeare play, attend a yoga class. Take piano or guitar lessons, and if you don't own an instrument, take voice lessons! The important thing is—don't find a reason not to.

Break the challenge into pieces so that success can be celebrated at each level.

If he's terrified of the dentist, just sitting in the waiting room for a few minutes on the first visit is enough. On the second visit, he can let the dentist look in his mouth. On the third visit, show the dentist how he brushes his teeth. Bryce's dentist told me Bryce, now a star patient, was the toughest nut he ever had to crack, but Dr. Mike had the patience of a saint. And he started with sitting on the floor in the hall outside the office with Bryce.

Make sure your child is properly equipped for the experience.

Make sure the skates are the right size, she won't be too hot or too cold, the instructions are phrased for her understanding.

Having a Plan B (and C and D) is smart planning and means you can move smoothly if problems arise.

But don't fall back on it unless it's truly necessary. If you look for problems, you will surely find them, even where they don't really exist. If you are fearful or anxious, be assured your child will pick up on it. Don't talk about your own fears unless it is in the framework of telling him how you faced and overcame those doubts.

As parents of these exceptional kids, we are not immune to fears and risks encountered in raising and loving them. Never does that risk seem more contradictory to me than when Bryce succeeds in reaching a milestone and it's time to let go. I'm getting better at it, but I have found letting go to be horridly hard because, when you have worked as hard as I have with Bryce, there is a twinge of self-pity in the jubilation over his independence. "He doesn't need me (as much, anymore, whatever qualifier)." After investing so much time, tears and spirit-draining energy in this worthwhile cause, when you succeed you are faced with a bit of void to fill. It's a little hollow area in your soul, kind of like the space in your mouth when each baby tooth falls out—it's open and bloody for a little while and your tongue keeps going over there to examine the wound, whether you want to or not. But pretty soon it heals over and eventually the hole is filled with something stronger ... and permanent.

"Pay no attention to that man behind the curtain!" Remember how very, very surprised Dorothy was to find out that the fearsome, larger-than-life, flame-and-smoke-belching wizard was really just an ordinary guy? That which appears so intimidating is not always what it seems. And even though the Wizard was in fact a fraud, the risks he forced Dorothy and her companions to face brought them full realization of the considerable extent of their own inner resources.

Only in their journey outside the safety of their familiar farmhouse, corn field and forest did they discover they were capable of much more than they had previously dared to dream. Your own expedition through autism is like that. It does not mean you are unafraid. It means that you heed the call of "courage that has said its prayers." You understand the risks yet forge ahead anyway, knowing and trusting that the prevailing winds of reward are going to shift unmistakably in your direction.

Solving the Behavior Equation

BEHAVIOR IS ALWAYS AT THE FOREFRONT OF DISCUSSIONS ABOUT THE child with autism: dragons, pirates, space aliens, mummies and terminators all rolled into one. Behavior discussions, whether between family members or between parent and school, are frequently supercharged. The issues vex and perplex. The origins are mystifying, the solutions elusive. Finding those solutions can mean having to go into potentially uncomfortable places that make unique demands upon us as parents and teachers.

In recent years I've become increasingly fascinated with how neurotypical adults respond to the challenging behaviors that our children present. I've observed a very wide spectrum of responses to this spectrum disorder and its spectrum of behaviors. Too often, what I see is that we fail to recognize that behavior always has a source, and far too often, we display a fatal lack of curiosity about that source, about what is causing those troubling behaviors. At worst, we make the assumption that the child could change this behavior at will if only he wanted to. Only slightly better are halfway efforts to address these behaviors by attempting to interrupt or extinguish them, squashing the symptom but disregarding the underlying reason for the behavior.

Not only is behavior one of autism's most discussed, debated and dreaded issues within and beyond the special needs category, but it is perhaps the most misunderstood as well. And yet the beginnings of taming the behavior beast come down to one simple concept: *All* behavior is communication. Your child or student is giving you information about factors seen or unseen in his environment that are affecting his ability to cope with any number of any issues: overwhelmed sensory system, impaired language functioning, emotional or physiological issues, social expectations. He is telling you that his so-called "negative" behavior is preventable, but only if you are willing to root out and address the cause.

And there is a reciprocal factor at work here too. What is your behavior telling him? It's the second part of an unavoidable two-part question: your own behavior is information you are giving your child about his environment.

Dr. Cliff Arnall, a British psychologist specializing in seasonal disorders, has calculated that January 24th is the most depressing day of the year. By that time, holiday cheer is gone, the bills are coming in, the weather is either the coldest or hottest of the year (depending upon hemisphere) and … most New Year's resolutions have already fallen by the wayside. This statement is a powerful reflection on us adults and our attempts at modifying our own behavior. In my book, *Ten Things Your Student With Autism Wishes You Knew,* I write:

> I urge you to be as gentle in your efforts to change your student or child's behavior as you could reasonably expect of yourself. It strikes me as sheer lunacy how much we expect of our students with autism in the area of behavior modification when we as adults find it so difficult to accomplish ourselves. Every darn New Year's, out come the same tired old behavior-modification resolutions: lose weight, stop smoking, spend less money, exercise more. By the end of January, it's usually all over

> but the shouting. What real right do we have to expect greater inner fortitude of a child living with perpetual neurological challenge than we are able to muster ourselves?
>
> The thing is, we frequently set ourselves up for failure because three or four New Year's resolutions are too many. We all know too well how demoralizing it is to swallow the fact that we didn't keep any of those resolutions, *didn't manage to change our behavior.* How much better it would be to pick one winnable battle at a time, to experience incremental success and the feeling of self-worth that comes with it before moving on to the next battle.

So approach the equation as seen through your child's eyes: behavior = you + me + environment. You may have read far and wide on the subject of behavior modification, but how much of what you've read asks you to focus not just on the child's behavior, but in equal part on your own adult behavior and the role it plays? If you can accept that your child's behavior may be a response to your own behavior, here is some food for thought, some ways we can begin to turn the tide.

Are you making a bad situation worse?

Believe this: your child truly does not want the spirit-crushing feedback he gets from "bad behavior," nor does he intentionally melt down, lash out or otherwise disrupt family or classroom. Ask yourself honestly if your response to his "bad behavior" is prolonging rather than resolving the crisis. Raising your voice means he hears the volume and tone, the anger and the scorn, but not the words. Trying to shame or embarrass him out of a behavior, letting him "learn a lesson the hard way," teaches only that he cannot trust you to protect him and guide him respectfully. Imposing a double standard, making him publicly follow rules that are different for him than for peers or siblings squashes his self-esteem and only makes it harder for him socially. Comparing his character or efforts to that of a sibling or other student is unfair and irrelevant.

At one time or another, we all make decisions in the heat of the moment that we later regret. If you do lose it, you can still produce a positive result by modeling how a responsible, compassionate and fully human person issues a sincere apology. He needs to learn that *everyone* makes mistakes, even you, but that we can also do a lot to make things right again, even when the mistake seems enormous.

When Plan A isn't working, move on to Plan B.

Perhaps you've heard Benjamin Franklin's oft-quoted definition of insanity: doing the same thing over and over and expecting different results. If despite your repeated efforts, your child's or student's behavior isn't changing, maybe the behavior that needs to change is yours. If his behavior hasn't changed, you haven't yet found the underlying unmet need that is the root cause. Look further. When your message isn't getting through, the burden is on you to change the message or a try different channel of communication.

Are your rewards really rewards?

Children with autism tend to have a narrow range of interests. Your child's interests may not be the same as those of his age-group peers. Assuming that he will find typical rewards motivating is a mistake. Bryce is a walking case study, having spent his lifetime being offered rewards that have no meaning to him. Over the years in school, sports or summer reading programs, he's been "rewarded" with things like McDonald's coupons (he is a devotee of the film *Supersize Me,* and never eats at McDonald's), Jolly Ranchers, candy canes and LifeSavers (dislikes all hard candy), Power Ranger/X-Men or similar branded paraphernalia relating to characters or TV shows, in whom he had no interest. Being rewarded for good behavior with "treats" your child hates (ice cream hurts my teeth!) or toys he doesn't understand (glad *you* like MLB Trivial Pursuit) will not inspire change. If you want to know what rewards your child or student will find motivating, ask! And if he isn't able to tell you in words, observe. What gets his interest, what makes him smile, what calms him, what excites him?

Walk your talk.

Be the model of what you want to see in him. If you yell, mock or hit when you are mad, he will too. If you are going to try to stop a repetitive behavior such as rocking, tapping or twirling, you can't expect her to understand why while you're chugging all those Diet Cokes or lattes, cracking your knuckles or your gum, jingling your keys, smoking, biting your nails, chewing the end of your pencil, snapping your watchband, tugging your cuffs or any one of hundreds of nervous habits we "typical" adults exhibit. Want him to learn not to interrupt and to pay attention to you when you talk? Double-check to make sure you are giving him the same courtesy.

Is the behavior harmful, or just annoying to you?

Behaviors that affect health or disrupt the classroom or home should be first priority. Then please give some thought to other behaviors you find "inappropriate" or "negative." I know, that incessant hair-twirling or tongue-clicking really dances on your third nerve. But of what real importance is it in the face of all he is ... facing? Health and safety issues trump mere irritations every time. Carefully consider, choose your battles, and focus your efforts where they will have the greatest benefit, one thing at a time.

Three centuries before the concept of autism spectrum disorders emerged, Sir Isaac Newton described the behavior equation perfectly in his Third Law of Motion: for every action there is an equal and opposite reaction. Or, turn it around: every reaction is caused by an equal (to your child) and opposite action. This kind of built-up pressure is what launches that all-time favorite science project, the bottle rocket. Behavior issues can seem about that volatile! But you have control of this rocket's trajectory. Your words, your attitude, your actions and your reactions are determining factors in your child's environment and his response to it. Only when we take a clear-eyed look at our own behavior will we have a chance of positively impacting our children's.

So Many Books, So Little Time

"When Jamie was first diagnosed with autism, I read everything I could get my hands on."

I hear this phrase almost as often as I hear "Good morning." It invariably comes from loving, devoted parents determined to do whatever is necessary to help their child with autism. They are irresistible forces planting their feet in front of the immovable object. They bravely confront the slenderness of the passage between the rock and the hard place. No matter how Big and Bad the Wolf, he is not gonna blow their house down. But after reading everything they can get their hands on, they often feel far from enlightened or educated. They are exhausted, confused, frustrated, bewildered—and paralyzed by information overload.

I've been there myself. When Bryce was first identified with autism, I too read everything I could get my hands on. There was much less to read back then, and all of what I read was either very clinical or very discouraging. I simply did not buy that my son was headed for residential care and a life of assembling widgets in a thingamabob factory. I did not buy that the way to teach him socially appropriate behavior was to spray water in his face when he "got it wrong" and give him an M&M when he "got it right."

I did not buy very many books. In fact, I stopped reading autism books altogether. During this time we had wonderful, knowledgeable teachers and therapists from whom I learned much. It was a full five years before I read another autism book. By then I wanted to write my own book and needed to know what was out there. I began reading again and what I found was that in those five years, the tide had turned. Many more understandable and encouraging books with practical, hands-on advice were being written by doctors, therapists, parents, and more. Today, the panoply of books on autism can overwhelm. Amazon.com's autism category contains over 11,000 listings.

So now many parents face a problem opposite from what I faced ten years ago—too much information—and yet end up in the same place, not being able to find the right information. Being an author, there's nothing I fear more than seeing one of my books on the dollar table at our library's annual used book sale—the ultimate statement that it wasn't useful. I take note of what shows up again and again on the wasn't-useful dollar table. There are a lot of cookbooks, diet books, exercise books and sure-cure books, flash-in-the-pan solutions that ultimately didn't work for the majority of their readers. And there are piles of Book-of-the-Month selections that didn't live up to the hype, didn't stir the reader enough to pass it to a friend as "recommended."

With our finite dollars and even more finite time, we want to do what we can to avoid future dollar-table dwellers. Choosing the autism book that will be helpful to you is a tricky balancing process. Cost is always a factor, as is available reading time. Your specific needs will ebb and flow over the course of your child's development, both as it pertains to autism and in the course of his typical development. Do you want a book to further your own knowledge, or to give to others, to in effect speak for you? Are you looking for hard information or divine inspiration? Perhaps both, but not simultaneously. So many factors to consider—I found myself amused by the fact that it took me almost a small book's worth of advice to write this column on how to choose a book!

The factors you consider will come and go over time, may be different each and every time you choose a book. But there are guideposts you can follow.

How much and what type of information you need in the immediate moment?

Where are you on the autism journey? Do you need an encyclopedic overview of all issues within autism? If your child has just been diagnosed, you might choose a comprehensive book that provides a little bit about everything. Every bookshelf needs one or two of these. Use these as reference tools, referring back to segments as needed and as new issues crop up.

If you are past the initial diagnosis, you may want to narrow your focus to deal with a specific issue. Social skills? Eating problems? Fine motor difficulties? Choose a smaller book by a more specialized author.

There are no one-size-fits-all solutions.

Any book that doesn't take into account the fact that each child, parent and family is unique and individual will ultimately fail. Programs that prescribe parameters that are too narrow, offer too little choice or flexibility within the formula for success, aren't adaptable to the multiple settings in which we live our lives are doomed to be short-lived. Ditto for anything that claims to be the last or only solution you will ever need. So ...

Test-drive the book.

- Cast a cautious eye on the book that espouses something "works for everyone" with ASDs. It doesn't, and even if it did, it doesn't mean that it is right for your family. A certain diet or program may in fact have great benefit for your child, but if it is going to make you crazy to administer it, bankrupt the family budget or throw the rest of the family into neglect or chaos, then it is not the right approach for you. Pre-educate yourself a little bit before buying such a book; do some internet research on the basics of that special diet or therapy. The intervention may be successful, but may require large amounts of time, patience and tenacity. If your initial reaction to the approach is a flicker of "Hey, that could work!" then proceed past Go. If your initial reaction is exhaustion at the thought of administering such a program, move on to something better suited to your lifestyle and temperament.

- Whenever possible, borrow the book from a library, school or social service agency to see if you truly will use it or enjoy it. If you can't borrow the book, apply this test in the bookstore: open the book in three random places. If you don't see anything that strikes a chord with you in three random spots, chances are the book is not for you.

- Make use of internet options for exploring a book. For instance, if you go to the Amazon.com listing for any of my books, you can read as many as 60 reviews, then use the Search Inside feature to read an excerpt, review the Table of Contents, flip through the index, and read the back cover. You'll have a good grasp of the format, tone, and content of the book without laying down a dime.

Don't be swayed by celebrity alone.

Celebrities are only flesh-and-blood parents like the rest of us, with one major difference—they usually have more money. More money means more freedom to try many different approaches, hire outside help, travel to distant hospitals and programs. Realistically, most of us must take a more limited and considered approach. Many of us will also give up much, including glamorous or not-so-glamorous career opportunities, in order to devote more time and energy to the needs of a child with autism. Will you be discouraged or misled if a celebrity implies that you can "have it all" (i.e., every increment of the career you want plus a successful child with autism)? It may or may not be true—beware.

Memoirs: uplifting or disheartening?

Memoirs can be inspiring and exhilarating, or they can be depressing provokers of excess stomach acid. When choosing to read a memoir, ask yourself what you want out of it. Do you want to identify or connect with someone in a situation similar to yours, regardless of whether you find solutions to the problems you both face? Do you expect the writer to provide you with usable practical wisdom? Will you compare your child to the writer's, and be unhappy if the comparison is not favorable? The 2006 James Frey-Oprah Winfrey flap brought to light the fact that, legally speaking, memoirs need not be 100% true. Are you okay with reading a "true" story that might be somewhat embroidered?

What's your reading *modus operandi*?

Do you want to explore alternative methodologies, or are you more comfortable going down a tested path already well trodden by others? What type of author draws you in? The parent writing from personal experience, the professional who has worked with thousands of kids, or the person with autism/Asperger's writing from the insider's perspective? All are valuable but you may prefer one voice over others.

Latest craze or core issue?

Is the book about the newest trend in therapy or thought, or does it address one of the hallmark challenges of autism? Keeping abreast of emerging information is important, but there are only so many hours in the day, which leads to ...

How much time do you have to read?

Be realistic—if it's only an hour a week, select a shorter book that gives you broad information on a topic. That way, you'll know what to hone in on next. If you have more time, go for something with more depth.

Let others help.

Are you lucky enough have a family member or friend who asks, what can I do to help? Give these good people a book or let them choose one. He or she can read it and then provide you with an overview/synopsis. This is such a win-win: a way for family to help you, while they themselves become further educated, too. It can't help but be a bridge to more meaningful relationships all the way around.

A book club can be a powerful tool.

A book club can be a powerful tool for getting a broad sweep of information from multiple books when time is precious. The usual book club format has everyone reading the same book and then discussing it in a once-a-month meeting. If that format appeals to you, great. But if it sounds like only more time pressure, create an alternative that better suits your lifestyle. Your reading circle, comprised of you and a few other parents or teachers of kids on the spectrum, can be a more efficient variation on that popular format.

- Instead of everyone reading the same book, each reads a different book and shares the information and his/her personal impressions with the rest of the group.
- Sharing of information can be through conventional face-to-face meetings, or virtual, through group emails, round robin emails or postings on a website.
- Members may decide to loan each other books based on information shared during meetings.

- Members may decide to pay annual or semi-annual money (say, $20) into a kitty used to purchase agreed-upon books for a group library. Members can agree to replenish the kitty as needed.

Rely on reliable authors.

If you still haven't a clue where to start, the autism category does have its core of reliable, knowledgeable authors to whom readers return again and again. Tony Attwood, Temple Grandin, Jed Baker, Brenda Smith-Myles, Carol Gray, Michelle Winner and Carol Kranowitz gain that national attention and recognition for a reason—their books are worth reading.

Cut your losses.

If you began eating a meal that tasted bad, bored you, or disagreed with you, would you force yourself to finish it? I hope not! The same goes for books. Beginning a book does not obligate you to finish it. Our reading time is finite, and the world is brimming with books begging for our attention. If a book doesn't capture your interest in the first few chapters, move on without a backward glance. This is why the library and other lending venues are invaluable. If you've bought a book you don't like, it's possible that it will be helpful later. It's also possible it would be helpful to someone else right now, so consider passing it on to those invaluable libraries and lending venues.

And finally ...

Beware burnout.

You can't read about autism all the time, especially when you are living with it all the time. Sometimes you need to "be" somewhere else, even if only figuratively. Sometimes you need to read just for fun. Whether it's a humorous novel, romance, mystery or cookbook, make some room in the reading schedule for *you*.

Books are so very important to the learning process, in a manner that no TV program, DVD or film will ever be able to touch: The exquisitely personal pictures you create in your head as you relate what you are reading to your own, real-time life. The portability of it—being able to take advantage of learning/reading moments whenever they present themselves at the laundromat, the park bench, the airplane or the bathroom. The permanence and the reliability of it—the same words will be there for you whenever you decide you need to revisit them, be it next week, next year or next child. My own autism writing career was more or less ignited by the fact that my child didn't relate to books—any books. The panic and the search for answers that it set off in me was the basis for several articles in both academic and family-oriented publications. Somewhere between his near-complete moratorium on books and my near-complete burial under an avalanche of current books lies the happy, healthy medium.

Special thanks to my friend, editor and co-author Veronica Zysk, Managing Editor of Autism Asperger's Digest, *whose thoughts on this subject contributed significantly to this piece.*

Seven Pillars of Wisdom

"Wisdom has built her house.
She has carved out her seven pillars."

PROVERBS 9:1

FINALLY! YOU'RE ABOUT TO READ AN ARTICLE ABOUT NEW YEAR'S resolutions that doesn't put forth one syllable about losing weight, saving money or organizing your closet. You know, one memorable year I did lose the weight and salt cash away. On the following January 1st, I was sitting there, faced with having to organize my closets. It was too ugly. I was forced to gain back the weight and spend some money.

Many of those all-knowing studies and statistics tell us that most New Year's resolutions fall by the wayside by the end of January. Perhaps we set too many goals; perhaps we set the goal too high. Perhaps we just don't see the relevance of the sheep mentality, turning over a new leaf based on some arbitrary calendar page. I always thought part of the problem was the word itself. Re-solution. Like retread, rehash, repeat or redo? Re-visiting the same problems in the same ways, getting meager (if any) results. That's crazy. No wonder it doesn't work—for you, or for your child.

This year, toss those stale no-solution resolutions in favor of something more concrete: New Year's affirmations to live by year in and year out. And remember—any day is the start of a new year. Even if you never lose a pound.

1. Live in the moment.

We've all done it: let ourselves slip into wondering what our lives would be like if our child didn't have autism. It's hard not to think about the "typical" experiences that are bypassing our family. But life isn't some hand of five-card stud where we can throw back a few of our cards in hopes of drawing something better. Nor is it a first draft that we can edit until we get the nuances just right. We play out the hand we drew in real time. Don't let if-onlys or what-I-could-have-done-differentlys thieve precious bits of your life away.

I had my mother's example to live by in this regard; she has an unshakeable belief in not dwelling on what-might-have-beens. I frequently quote poet John Greenleaf Whittier, who summarized it eloquently when he wrote:

For of all sad words of tongue or pen,
The saddest are these: "It might have been!"

Living in the moment means focusing less on getting what you want and more on wanting what you already have. The lesser-known part of Whittier's poem goes on to say "God pity us all, who vainly dream...." Personally, I have a visceral reaction to being on the receiving end of pity. Never wanted it for my situation, and that goes double for my children. But the operative word in Whittier's phrase is "vainly." Living in the moment doesn't mean not planning for the future, not having goals, not having a dream. It means embracing the goal and the dream that is in fact achievable, and trusting yourself and the *process* of working towards those goals and dreams enough that you can enjoy and cherish the irreplaceable here-and-now moments that are beautiful in their own right. Author Katherine Mansfield put it more bluntly that Whittier. "Regret," she said, "is an appalling waste of energy. You can't build on it; it's only for wallowing in."

2. Be a cliché.

Slow and steady *does* win the race: see # 5, and realize that instant results usually dissipate just as quickly. An ounce of prevention *is* worth a pound of cure: see # 7. There *is* no use in crying over spilt milk: see # 1, and repeat as necessary, "lamenting past events only saps me of the energy to look forward and have an effect on what hasn't happened yet."

3. Don't be a cliché.

There *are* things to fear besides fear itself—ignorance and bigotry, for instance; but fearing something does not mean you will not confront it. All good things will *not* come to those who wait, unless you are actively working towards those good things—like social competence and independent living skills—while you are waiting. Just because you cannot beat them does *not* mean you should join them. Better to go out and find yourself some "thems" to join whose values, worldview and work ethic are more closely aligned with yours.

4. Don't therapize your child.

Of course therapies are essential. My reverence for occupational and speech therapy borders on religious. But we should not fill all our child's hours with all manner of adults trying to "fix" or do something to him. Think about the message this sends to a child. Learning to laugh, play, explore and build connections with others is just as important as any therapy, and it does not happen behind the doors of a clinic.

5. Look for increments rather than earthquakes.

I cringe every time I hear a parent or teacher talk about hoping to achieve a "breakthrough." Autism is challenging enough without adding expectations infused with this kind of drama. Much more likely is that your child will progress in increments, perhaps so small you don't detect them individually, but one day realize the collective result. Going from four meltdowns a day to two is what retailers call a big reduction—50% off! Going from not being able to tolerate restaurants to being able to handle thirty minutes in a no-waiting buffet-style diner is also big stuff—it's not the leisurely meal at the venue of your choice, but it's a stop on the way there.

Here's a great way to visualize those increments. Hang onto a few of those hokey promotional calendars you get every December. Jot just a few words on the days your child does something new and noticeable, however small—says hello to a neighbor at the store, tries a new food, new shirt, new game, new word. Goes a day (or an hour) without screaming, swearing, crying. The bits of time you invest recording these small moments return big results. Soon you will be able to look back across a day-by-day affirmation of progress.

Extend this to yourself, too. Take another one of those hokey calendars and record your own incremental successes—the mountains *and* the molehills you climb, the truths and the fictions you uncover. This calendar will be your new best friend, the branch overhead on the days that feel like quicksand, wheels spinning, ooze closing in.

6. Recognize and reject futility.

We had a very odd feathered friend in our previous neighborhood. Our house had a metal chimney vent and every day a woodpecker came to drill his heart out on it, machine-gun style. He never learned that no matter how tenacious and persistent his efforts, he was never going to penetrate that metal and find grubs underneath.

The definition of insanity is doing the same thing over and over and expecting different results. If you've been devotedly, stalwartly banging away at an issue or situation and nothing has changed, it's time to move on to Plan B. Do it without bitterness or defeatism; do it with an attitude of "Okay, Plan A didn't work so now it's on to Plan B. Thank goodness I have a Plan B!" And speaking of which ...

7. Always have a Plan B.

It may seem exhausting to have to come up with a contingency for every turn the days and months may take, but I assure you of two things: 1) with practice, it will become second nature, and 2) it will save you untold grief and mayhem in the long run. No matter how large or small the event or task, if you also have the backup plan and the exit strategy, you will never find yourself desperate or blindsided. If you can learn to accept the day-to-day challenges of autism with a certain level of objectivity, you will Pass Go flying and never have to do time in the penitentiary of frustration, exasperation and self-pity.

Mark Twain tells us that January 1st "is the accepted time to make your regular annual good resolutions. Next week you can begin paving hell with them as usual." But that's not us, is it? Because we are not a cliché—at least not that one! This is the year your road less traveled can be paved not just with good intentions, but with good attitude, gratitude and the satisfaction of actual achievement.

Even if your closets are still a mess.

Rx for Battle Fatigue

AFTER YOU'VE BEEN TO A FEW HUNDRED WHITE-TABLECLOTH BUSINESS dinners, the food and the deal points change, but otherwise they are all pretty much the same. This one was ambling along that way, until the conversation veered off the path.

I'm sick of hearing about ADHD, announced the neatly pressed executive across the table. It's nothing more than a convenient excuse for parents who don't have the guts to discipline their children.

Interesting, I reply. And is your experience clinical or practical?

I beg your pardon? He blinks at me blankly.

Clinical or practical? I persist. Do you work with these children, or are you parenting one? Are you a doctor, a psychologist, a teacher, a professional of some sort? Or do you live with a child with ADHD?

Oh, no, no, no, he says with a smug shake of the head. None of that. It's just what I think.

And here's what I think, I told him. I have thousands of hours and thousands of dollars invested in living with and attempting to understand, care for, educate and protect such a child. And the many devoted professionals with whom we work year in and year out possess a body of factual knowledge strongly supporting that "what you think" is uninformed, unkind and judgmental. People like you make me more tired than an entire room full of hyperactive kids.

My response was admittedly one of exasperation, and since then I have come a long way in my ability to respond in a more productive fashion to such situations. But that was where I was at that moment—one step short of giving him my favorite snappy comeback, the raising of three fingers together and telling him to read between the lines. (I've actually only used that one once, but knowing it's in the arsenal makes me smile.) I don't remember if I blew the business deal that night, but it never occurred to me that it wasn't worth it. There were six people at that table, and if I caused even the slightest flicker of an attitude shift in even one of them, the evening was profitable enough for me.

As parents of children with autism, the list of what makes us tired is endless. The meltdowns, the sleeplessness (theirs and ours), the siblings who don't get enough attention, the minutiae of preparation each outing requires, the grinding challenge of trying to adequately feed a child who only eats four things, the social isolation (theirs and ours), the endless carousel of service providers and how to pay for them. But nothing makes me more tired than perpetually jousting with a large portion of the general public who feels that children who qualify for special education are some sort of societal add-on, lacking in legitimacy and value, a drain on the system, and that money spent on special ed somehow inflicts injustice on the "typical" learner. This is a real live letter to the editor that appeared in our newspaper in 2005:

> Mainstreaming special needs children hurts all children. My kids have been in classrooms with some of the special-needs

> kids who really can't do the work and require so much time of the teacher that all the normal kids get lost in the shuffle.
>
> Our schools are failing the average student, who becomes the real burden to society. These are the kids who need help. Our schools are out of money now. What we don't need is to add more cost for a handful of "special people."
>
> I know it must be heartache for the parents of these kids, but if it means relocating to be closer to a facility that is better suited for their child, so be it. My heart goes out to these families, but I have even more compassion for the kids who are shuffled through the cracks.

I'll bypass the question of how this woman's heart could go out to anyone when she so clearly doesn't have one to begin with. Or how dangerous it is when we begin trying to define what a normal child is. As Canadian songwriter Bruce Cockburn put it, "the trouble with normal is it always gets worse."

Having to face the bigotry of an uninformed world-at-large comes with the territory of having a child with an autism spectrum disorder. There is no gel-tab available to help you swallow that. But you do have a choice about how you confront it. The menu from which you can choose includes anger, denial, despair, frustration. Or it could include patience, resilience and a willingness to view ignorance as opportunity.

Since the years-ago evening I told off Mr. Business Dinner, I've authored several books on raising a child with autism, and with that comes mail from readers. At least 99% of the mail I get is positive, but there is the occasional missive from someone who is very, very angry with me. Am I crazy, they ask, or just full of bull? How *dare* I voice such a viewpoint?

My husband never understands why I even respond to such vitriol, but I always do respond. Every point of contact is a break in the clouds, when both reader and writer can widen their perspective on the very perplexing, bottomless, and amorphous subject of autism. I counter in a thoughtful, respectful but heartfelt way that emphasizes how many different ways there are to approach the issues within autism, that there can be different answers for each different child, family and school, and that in our differences we are still pursuing the same end goal—that each child with autism achieve the fullest of his potential and be able to take his place in society as an adult carrying as much of his own weight as possible. I point out that this goal is no different from what most people want for their own "typical" children—and for themselves. Every time I get a return response along the lines of gee, I never thought of it that way or wow, I didn't know that—I know I did the right thing in putting myself in the line of fire and "taking one for the team."

There are acute differences of opinion within the autism community, and dealing with these alone can make you weary. But standing up to the ignorance of the general public can feel positively athletic; it requires Olympic endurance. Over the course of raising your child, you'll face a spectrum of responses just as wide and varied as autism itself: benign lack of information, open hostility, complete indifference, medieval thinking, Pollyanna thinking and everything in between. It gets a lot easier if you bear in mind at all times two things:

Knowledge is power.

You have the knowledge, therefore you have the power.

You have two kinds of knowledge, therefore you have two kinds of power. The obvious one is that you have knowledge about autism, factual information as well as your own firsthand experiences. That's the knowledge you use to counteract ignorance, misconception and prejudice in others. But even more powerful is the knowledge that you know your own child better than anyone else, and you know that the choices you've made in what you are doing and pursuing for him are the right ones. Hold fast to this knowledge in the face of that ignorance, misconception and prejudice, and you will not blow over, no matter how stiff the wind. *Trust your instincts,* our very first pediatrician told us. *You know more than you think you know.*

Another thing my husband doesn't quite understand is how I have been able to use this second kind of knowledge/power to overcome my anger at those who denigrate our efforts, and replace it with something resembling pity. It was hard and painful, but I was determined to do it. For one thing, anger is draining. My stamina is finite; I wanted to put it all into constructive efforts for my sons and not have to keep sticking my finger into little dikes dribbling rage and resentment. "Assholes do vex me!" was the motto of a long-ago young college professor friend of mine, and don't we all have moments wherein we agree! But I truly can say that I feel sorry for those who are not able to see beyond mean stereotypes, who leap to judgment without factual backup, who fear what they do not understand and who live with the constant anxiety that someone will take away their fair share of whatever is being divvied up or allocated. I'm glad I don't have to live life as that kind of person, because I think it would be much harder to recover from that sort of smallness than from autism—in spades.

Making a difference one person at a time makes a huge difference over time.

I'm happy winning over hearts and minds one by one because I have faith in the ripple effect. Maybe I wasn't able to participate in the autism walk-a-thon or write the big check to the fundraiser. But every person who walks away from me understanding just a bit more than he or she did before will likely share it with someone else who will, in turn, do the same. That sort of "passing the talking stick" ultimately makes life easier for my child, your child … and you and me!

Running the marathon that is raising your child with autism is almost certain to make you tired. But think about how many different ways there are to be tired. There's the tired that is laced with defeat, fear, and loneliness. And there is the tired that says, I gave it a good effort and look how far I got!

So I wrote back to the reader who berated aspects of my writings as "crazy," who said autism could never be seen as a gift, but "rather a curse."

I told her that the bedrock of my attitude is that the individual with autism is not a bundle of broken pieces but whole person, full of their own unique ideas, dreams, fears, preferences and quirks. "Autism does affect the way they think and the manner in which they respond to their environment, social and physical," I wrote. "But to characterize it as a 'curse' does not reflect the experience of every person with autism. Much of any individual outcome will be dependent upon educational, attitudinal and biomedical approaches taken by those providing care and guidance to the child with autism."

I described to her Bryce's journey, beginning at age three when he was nonverbal, sensory disordered, suffered daily meltdowns, and lacked age-appropriate social skills. Today, at fourteen, he is 4.0 student, plays team sports, acts in plays and film, dates, camps, surfs, cooks, does his own laundry, and is generally more capable and responsible than many teens much older than he is. "It's always interesting to hear the occasional person suggest that because he has done so well, maybe he didn't actually have autism to begin with," I told her. "The dozens of devoted teachers, therapists and family members who have worked with him over the years know better."

DSM-IV (Diagnostic and Statistical Manual of Mental Disorders) is only the beginning of the definition of autism, not the last word. By its very nature as a spectrum disorder, there can be no one correct approach. Whether or not we agree about the possibility that Mozart had autism is irrelevant. What is relevant is what we get up and do every day to help our children with autism move toward the satisfying, productive adulthood to which they are entitled. Some will make it; some won't. For each child, within either outcome, we have to look not only at the child but also at ourselves, and ask why.

I thanked my reader for sharing her thoughts. "I learn something from each and every one of my readers," I told her, "and I value that."

I did not expect a response, so I was greatly surprised when one arrived promptly.

Dear Ellen,

Thank you very much for considering my critique and giving me some food for thought. The story of your son really does amaze me. Probably a big part of his progress has been your positive attitude and I really admire that.

Maybe I've seen autists too much of a lost cause, but I am glad that reality proves me wrong.

Postcards from the Schoolroom

Our different learner thinks differently; absorbs, processes and retrieves differently. The delineation between teacher, student and parent blurs. Learner must teach, teacher must learn. Here, the three Rs are different: Respect, Reroute and Repeat. The ABCs are not an alphabet but an attitude. A—assume nothing, B—behavior speaks loudly and carries a big stick, C—communication, communication, communication. *Probe.*

Ready for K ... and Beyond

I still remember the prickle in my stomach when I read my son's final teacher report from preschool. "Takes responsibility for own actions. Functions well in a small group," it said. "Ready for K."

Ready for K. It might as well have said "ready for blast-off."

The transition to kindergarten is only the first of many transitions that will be part of your life until your child graduates high school and beyond. However, that first transition, to kindergarten, amounts to a shift of geologic proportions, a virtual Matterhorn of New and Unfamiliar. New school, new teachers, new bus, peers, routine, tasks and expectations. It's a major shift in focus from early childhood educational settings (preschools), where child development is encouraged through play; in kindergarten the emphasis shifts to academics. The class size to which your child is accustomed will likely increase significantly. She may have been attending preschool three or four times a week; now she will attend kindergarten five days a week. And if your little one is going from half-day preschool to full-day kindergarten, the longer hours alone may be a steep challenge.

Big changes are in store for you as well. With the move to kindergarten comes a huge change in educational approach: as a preschooler, your child had an IFSP—an Individual Family Service Plan. You probably met twice yearly with your teacher or caseworker to review goals. Once the child reaches school age, the document becomes an IEP—an Individual Education Plan. The school now serves only the child, not the family, and formal review is required only once a year. At the time, this came as quite a shock to me. I showed up for the IEP meeting with a request for help in addressing a troublesome behavior. Came good news/bad news the response: Bryce didn't exhibit that behavior at school. With no observational data backing up my claim, it could not be addressed in the IEP. I was on my own with that particular behavior. This is an not example of a bad school, but rather the realities of the law.

That reverberating thud I just heard was the sound of a few of you hitting the floor, right? Well, pick yourselves up. Even though it is over a decade since Bryce made his transition to kindergarten, it is vivid in my memory because it was, in spite of all my apprehension, smooth as silk. It *can* happen that way. I owe our soft landing to our genius of a preschool teacher. She knew just how critical these transitions are and gave me guidance that lasted me all through Bryce's childhood.

The most important consideration for this and all the transitions to come, for your child and for you, is: *no surprises*. OPCs (other people's children) may delight in surprises, but confronting the unexpected likely leaves your child distressed, distraught and disoriented. This is exactly why the element of surprise is a popular and effective tactic in war. For him as a learner and for you as his advocate, the more you both know about what to expect, minute by minute, the less anxiety both of you will experience and the quicker both of you will adjust.

No Surprises is a mighty useful mindset to develop right from the start because you will be astonished at how quickly minute-by-minute turns into day-to-day and year-after-year. The transition to kindergarten is huge, but there will also be transitions each year as your child passes to a new grade level, and ultimately on to middle school and high school. Unthinkable now—but come it does, and you want it to. It's the natural order.

No Surprises goes hand in hand with another favorite philosophy of mine, and that is ASSUME NOTHING. Assuming anything without hard facts is the equivalent of guessing. In a transition as significant as the move to kindergarten, even educated guesses aren't good enough. In the space of one column, I could never provide you with all the tools and guidance it would take to ensure that you could avoid every unpleasant surprise, but I can give you a place to start, and a place to come back to each year when you face yet another transition.

For Your Child

- Show and tell! Your child likely absorbs information most easily when it is visually presented. Photos and videos of a new school, new classroom, new teachers and staff, go a long way toward familiarizing your child with his new environment. Visit the new classroom, meet the new teacher one-on-one before the crush of the first day of school. Visual schedules in multiple settings will smooth many tasks. Class pictures and yearbooks help him connect to schoolmates.
- Enlist all school staff and peer buddies to be ever alert for non-academic obstacles that can derail his day. Especially beware the restroom, lunchroom, playground. If your little boy has a female paraeducator, you may be a long time finding out that he never washes his hands because he can't figure out the sink (foot pedal? motion sensor?) or the towel dispenser, or worse, "holds it" all day because he can't figure out the commodes or the lights. Then on to the lunchroom, where he goes hungry because he can't figure out the lunchbox clasp, the zip baggie, the juice box. And then to the playground, where he "walks the fence" because he doesn't know how to snag a basketball for himself. Is he perpetually time-

Show and Tell: The Social Story™

The Social Story as pioneered by Carol Gray, founder of the Gray Center in Kentwood, Michigan, is a powerful tool, and just right for the transition to kindergarten. A Social Story explains a potentially difficult situation, event or idea in a manner that affirms the child's ability to handle it by emphasizing his strengths, his interests and knowledge his already has. Introducing a new upcoming experience this way can make it seem like familiar routine before it ever even happens. The Gray Center provides excellent information on how to write a Social Story at *www.thegraycenter.org/socialstories.cfm* (address current as of September 2007).

Our Social Story, "My New Kindergarten," starring Bryce, was a humble production: large type text accompanied by photographs glued to the pages—that's it. It began with the positive statement, "I get to go to kindergarten." The next pages introduced him to his new teachers and school staff, his new classroom, playground, gym, cafeteria. It included photos of old friends who would go with him to the new school. It ended with the affirmation that "I will like my new school." We read our simple little book many times throughout the summer, and when the big day came, Bryce found that he did indeed like his new school quite a lot.

disoriented because the school clocks are all analog, and he is used to digital only?

Some years ago, someone strapped a camera to the President Bush's dog and made a little video about Christmas at the White House from the dog's ankle-high viewpoint as the terrier scurried from room to room. I can just hear my wonderful father, who loved people but not dogs, saying "this rates *two* fingers down the throat!" But the concept is a good one: seeing the world from the actual vantage point of someone smaller and with different issues than your own. Walking through your child's school day with a camcorder held at his eye level might give you startling insights, allowing you to anticipate and address problems before they occur. Doing this before the first day of school, not only gives him a run-through of the routine but gives both of you important visual information about his new environment. You can then use the summer to identify and practice skills that will assure a smooth transition, doing it in the safe haven of home rather than in front of a potentially humiliating audience of peers.

- You may not be the one leading the book circle or handing out the spelling list, but you are a teacher too. You are the teacher who doesn't go home for weekends and holidays and who doesn't pass from his life at the end of each school year. Right from the start, begin to teach him the self-reliance that will support him in his adulthood, however far away that may seem. It comes much sooner than you could ever dream; a wise friend of mine once commented, "The days last forever but years fly by." This is so true, as in the crush of our daily routine, it seems so much more expedient to find his lost library book for him, finish his homework, tie his shoes, pour his cereal. But learning to navigate his day and his world independently will only happen through patient repetition, so build that extra time into your daily routine and remind yourself that, in this regard, your job is to instruct, not intervene.

For You

- *Do not assume* that all pertinent records and reports will make their way to a new school or new teacher each year. *Do not assume* that the new teacher will have read them even if received. Confer as early in the process as possible to ensure that she does have adequate background information on your child and adequate training in teaching children with ASD. If you end up having to be the one to gather and disseminate this information, do it in the spirit of teamwork, not combat. Most teachers truly do have your child's best interests at heart, even when they are severely restricted by school resources, class load, or inadequate training.
- As mentioned earlier, *do not assume* that you will receive the same level and type of service in an IEP (Individualized Education Program) that you may have received in an IFSP. If you haven't already, familiarize yourself with the major special education laws that pertain to school age children.
- *Do not assume* that you will have unlimited access to the classroom or to school records. Each teacher, school and parent is different. Not all moms can volunteer in the classroom, not all kids want their moms there, and not all teachers have open-door poli-

cies. Explore all the ways you can be involved with the school community, through site councils, advisory boards, PTA, web rings and listserves.

- Good teacher, bad teacher. *Do not assume* that the next teacher or school will duplicate your previous experience. Each new teacher and school deserves to start with a clean slate and build a relationship with you that is based on fact, not second-guesses or preconceived notions.
- *Do not assume* your child can or will tell you what is happening at school. A home-school communication book that goes back and forth each day will circumvent an untold number of nasty surprises on both ends.

For the Big Picture:

Do not assume that your neighborhood school is your only option, let alone the best option for your child. This is not a for-better-or-worse marriage, but a case of situational geography, and it does not preclude your exploring the possibility of a better placement, a better fit for your child. As part of your transition program, you should become aware, either through the district's instigation or your own initiative, of all opportunities open to your child, including intradistrict transfer (with or without transportation provided), charter schools, magnet programs, special education clusters. We made the decision to move at the end of preschool when it became evident that our neighborhood school was not special education-friendly. Had we not had the wherewithal to move—and moving is a huge proposition with transition issues of its own—I would have ferociously pursued intradistrict transfer to the school we chose.

Choosing the right school is important because every year, your child will face transition to the next grade. A school that emphasizes teamwork among its staff will just naturally serve your child better during these potentially bumpy times. As parents, it's not possible for us to control the variables that go into running a school, but there are a couple of indicators that provide a good barometer. First, look at the average tenure of the staff. Low turnover doesn't guarantee there won't be any in the future, but it's probably an indication of a good working environment. One of Bryce's teachers, new to the school, was delighted to observe that staff met each day for lunch for the purpose of sharing information and problem-solving—a startling change from her previous school where teachers spent lunch hour grousing.

Second, try to get a feel for whether special education learners are regarded as full members of the school community, or inconveniences. Is the resource room in the heart of the school, or tucked away in a back corner? Would your child's caseworker be the general education classroom teacher, or someone with expertise in autism? What level of school-home communication is the staff willing to provide? If the school has discretionary dollars in its budget, ask how they are spent. We ultimately chose a school that spent its discretionary dollars on a child development specialist staff position while one nearby school used the money for a school orchestra. Another opted for a soccer team. We felt that such choices benefited only a small percentage of the student body, neither of which included our child.

Off and Running

Having said all this, it should be evident that you do not want to be turning the calendar over to May and just starting to think about school transitions. That is when all the pieces should be in place and you are turning the ignition and saying, "let's roll." To paraphrase Richard Daley: think early, think often. January is not too soon to begin the process. Assembling and distributing all the necessary documentation, ensuring that staff has all pertinent information on your child, including successful teaching techniques and materials—it all takes a grinding amount of time, even in the best of schools. Be realistic—your child is only one of a teacher's caseload that may run into the dozens. Allowing adequate time for all to prepare is the only sensible place to start.

"Ready for K." If this transition feels stressful to you as well as your child, know that you are not alone. At a good school, staff knows that transition can be stressful for Mom as well as child. I simply melted with gratitude every year as I watched what our school did for first-day kindergarten parents. All are invited to leave their child at the classroom and then come to the library—for coffee and Kleenex. "It's normal to break out into tears when you leave your child for the first time in the big public school," says the ever-wise Leslie, our school secretary of many years. "It's easier if parents can go to the 'crying room' together and share laughs, tears and stories. It's just part of a child's growing up—and we know that's hard for parents sometimes too."

While the law mandates the number of required IEP meetings, you have the right to request a meeting at any time you have concerns about any facet of the IEP. I've called mid-year meetings when I felt goals had been achieved and new ones were needed, when home-school communication regarding progress on goals was not adequate, when I didn't feel the teaching methodology was autism-specific enough. In a good school, teachers want this feedback from you. The Division for Early Childhood presented data at its 2005 national conference noting that the two barriers to smooth kindergarten transition most frequently cited by teachers are parents not reading letters and other information that is sent home, and parents being generally uninvolved in the transition process.

When Math Doesn't Add Up

WHEN IT COMES TO SCHOOL, ANYTHING WITH THE WORD "STANdardized" in front of it really, really sets me off. Standardized testing, standardized assessment, standardized lessons and worksheets. Common sense should tell any educator or any parent that most one-size-fits-all learning materials directed at the general population will require modification in order to be appropriate for a child with autism. And yet, year after year I fight my way through a quagmire of inappropriate tests and lessons on behalf of my children. "Math Suks!" warbles Jimmy Buffett's famous song. My son Bryce might agree, except upon closer examination, it's probably not math that "suks," but the unsuitable manner in which it is sometimes presented and from which he is expected to learn.

In this column, a "typical" math worksheet is going to stand trial in the court of Autism-Appropriate Education, Judge Ellen presiding. Court is held in a swamp of ambiguity, and it will be an eye-opening trip for a lot of adults who simply don't take our kids' language struggles into account. The exhibit: the actual worksheet Bryce received on the first day of school one year. It nearly paralyzed him, and not because he can't add and subtract; of course he can. But, as I explained to the teacher who had just met him for the first time: "Bryce's autism manifests most strongly in his moderate to severe language deficits. He struggles particularly hard with the language involved in math. As such we must be very specific about teaching the functions of math with as little language complication as possible. This worksheet is a minefield of unnecessary and unclear language."

Exhibit A: 5th Grade Math Worksheet
Addition and Subtraction
Directions: Add or subtract to find the answers.

Problem 1: Eastland School hosted a field day. Students could sign up for a variety of events. 175 students signed up for individual races. Twenty two-person teams competed in the mile relay and 36 kids took part in the high jump. How many students participated in the activities?

- "Students could sign up for a variety of events" is unnecessary to the solving of the problem; it clutters up the relevant information.
- "Twenty two-person teams." Bryce read this, as many ASD students would, without the hyphen: 22, not 20 x 2. The directions tell him to "add or subtract to find the answer," but the text shifts in mid-problem, requires multiplication within the add-or-subtract operation. The directions are unclear, inconsistent, and nearly impossible for many ASD kids to follow.
- We don't really know how many students "participated" because some "competed" and some "took part," but some only "signed up."
- The worksheet is labeled Grade 5, but the Fleisch-Kinkaid Readability test rates this problem as Grade 9.

Here's the same problem rewritten in an autism-friendly manner that emphasizes math, not language, and includes only the relevant information: **At Eastland School Field Day, 175 students ran in individual races. 40 students ran in a relay race, and 36 kids did the high jump. How many students participated in Field Day?**

> **Problem 2:** The Booster Club sponsored a concession stand during the day. Last year, they made $1,000 at the same event. This year, they hoped to earn at least $1,250. They actually raised $1,842. How much more did they make than they anticipated?

- Again, a superfluous, unnecessary sentence confuses the problem. "Last year, they made $1,000" has no bearing on the calculation requested.
- The problem assumes an 8th grade vocabulary. How many children know what a "Booster Club" is? He is left to wonder: is it a club for people who need baby seats at restaurants? A club for people who need their tetanus shots? And why are we "earning" money in one sentence, but "raising" it in the next; is it going to levitate? A student cannot focus on the math part of the problem when he is baffled by the language.

In concrete, autism-friendly language, the problem might look like this: **A group of parents called The Booster Club sold snacks. They hoped to earn $1,250. They actually earned $1,842. How much more did they earn than they hoped to?**

> **Problem 3:** Each school was awarded a trophy for participating in the field day activities. The Booster Club planned to purchase three plaques as awards, but they only wanted to spend $150. The first place trophy they selected was $68. The second place award was $59. How much would they be able to spend on the third place award if they stay within their budgeted amount?

- "Each school" is awarded a trophy but we are not told how many schools were there. But it's irrelevant anyway, since the problem is asking only about awards for first, second, and third place.
- In the first sentence, reference is made to a "trophy." In the next sentence, it changes to "plaque," then it's back to "trophy" and in the fourth sentence it becomes an "award." All are referring to the same thing, but the math problem has now become an exercise in synonyms, obscuring the math intent.
- Fleisch-Kinkaid Readability test rates this problem as Grade 8.

Autism friendly wording: **The Booster Club had $150 with which to buy trophies for the teams finishing first, second and third place. The first place trophy they selected was $68. The second place trophy was $59. How much money was left to spend on the third place trophy?**

Problem 4: The Booster Club decided to spend $1,000 to purchase several items for the school with the money they had earned. Study the list of items suggested and decide which combination of items they could purchase.

A. Swing set $425

B. Sliding board $263

C. Scoreboard $515

D. Team uniforms $180

- The instructions say to "decide" which combinations of items are possible within the $1,000. (There are actually 8, given 2 and/or 3 item combinations!) And, it doesn't tell us how to express it. Even I couldn't figure how to record the answers once the calculations were complete. Students with ASD cannot and should not be required to infer what is required of them.
- Fleisch-Kinkaid Readability test rates this problem as Grade 11.

This assignment was far, far removed from being a fair evaluation of my son's math skills. It was an evaluation of his ability to decode the language of a poorly written standardized worksheet designed for a general population, one written at several grade levels above both his chronological age and even the purported grade level of the worksheet itself. That he is a student with autism with documented language challenges was not accommodated in this assignment.

Having to bird-dog stuff like this truly exhausts me. It "suks." But what is the alternative? Our children fall farther and farther behind in basic math, a necessary life skill for adult independence. Your child and mine may actually be quite competent at math, but given lessons like this one, we will never know.

Parents should not have to be responsible for correcting inappropriate educational materials, but at the least we may have to take an initiating role. Autism-specific education simply hasn't risen yet to the level where educators across the board are sufficiently aware of the invisible barriers our kids face. I don't believe for a minute that work like this is presented to our kids maliciously, out of laziness, or with indifference to the fact that it dooms them to failure. I believe we are looking at a true lack of awareness. Our school is an excellent one, and teachers have been more than willing to do whatever was needed for Bryce—but first they had to know what that was. In a perfect world, all teachers would be autism-trained. But in the real world—using our school as an example—the resource teacher has to sort out and administer twenty-nine IEPs spanning all sorts of disabilities, and she has only six teaching hours a day to do it. Her response, by the way, to my concerns about the worksheet could not have been more prompt.

The burden may well fall on you to educate school personnel about your child's needs in general, and how detrimental "typical" teaching materials can be for these students. The less cooperative the school district, the more you'll need to advocate for your child. Just as you do for your child when he's faced with any immense task, break it into smaller pieces.

- Review all schoolwork that comes home, both assignments in progress and work completed. Bring language problems to the teacher's attention. Do it consistently until the message is received and action applied.
- See that a section is added to your child's IEP specifying that language for all schoolwork be chunked down into smaller segments correspondent to her language competence.
- Ask for the school speech/language pathologist to work with teachers to create appropriate materials for your child.
- If you can, offer your assistance in modifying materials.
- Steady as she goes—you won't be able to tackle this problem across all subject areas in one fell swoop. Do it one assignment at a time. This is a marathon, not a sprint.
- When the task seems overwhelming, visualize the result you want: your child as an independent adult. Don't turn away from that vision. What you do now matters very much, not just for him, but for every child like him yet to come.

Directions: Add or subtract to find the answer.

A parent rewrote a standard math worksheet in a manner that helped her son with autism better understand it. Her son's resource teacher presented the information to seven teachers and the principal at a staff meeting. The principal presented the information to 45 other teachers at the next district in-service. Then he posted the information on the school website where it was read by 276 parents. How many people were helped by the work of one parent?

What Tiggers Do Best

"You can't bounce the bounce if you can't even pronounce the bounce."

TIGGER

"AND THAT'S WHY IT FREQUENTLY ALL FALLS APART IN MIDDLE school," concluded the special education administrator. He was speaking to me as both a professional and a parent. While I have two sons, one with ADHD and one with autism, he has one son with both "all rolled into one," proving once again that you can always find someone with greater challenges than your own. From his position on the observation deck of district-wide administration, he had noted that the nurturing culture embraced by most elementary schools tends to disappear at the middle school level. "Middle school teachers seem to want to treat their students as little adults," he said, "And of course they are not. But this level of expectation only makes things that much harder for the kids with ASDs."

The expectation of "little adulthood" hits ASD children so much harder because it has at its core one of the more difficult and enigmatic impairments of autism: Theory of Mind skills. These are the skills embodied in what we call critical thinking (classification, comparison, application), executive management (attention, planning and memory functions) and social pragmatics (perspective-taking), and they are largely missing from the thought processes of most children with autism. And if your child has high-functioning autism, as does my son Bryce, the lack of these invisible, intangible, unquantifiable skills can be hugely detrimental to learning. Many, if not most, teachers are not well-versed in how to teach to a student who lacks ToM skills, and may not even see it in a child who outwardly appears as competent as Bryce does.

Seventh grade was indeed a difficult year for Bryce. He not only was navigating the white water of normal adolescence, but also truly confronting his autism for the first time and having to face down the limitations it was trying to put on him. At the same time, the curriculum and assignments began to require an ever-increasing amount of abstract thought. Much more onerous than the factual aspects of world history or earth science were the confounding Theory of Mind requirements of the assignments: comparative perspective, inferential ability, generalization and reclassification skills needed to complete the work, and the cognitive and social agility to do it all in prescribed timeframes—sometimes independently, sometimes in small groups, sometimes along with the class as a whole.

It's not what you could call a strengths-based curriculum for the student with ASD, as it certainly wasn't for Bryce. Lucky it was for us the school's speech language pathologist, Christine, had a deep understanding of the core issues of autism and how they impacted Bryce. Their year together was challenging to be sure, but by June we could look back and see major progress. And now, almost another full year later, I'm astonished (for the umpteenth time) at how far Bryce has come, with her guidance, in developing those skills.

"For children identified with learning disabilities," says Christine, "as many as 80% of those difficulties are language-based. Students don't always end up with a speech pathologist even though they may be struggling with reading, writing or even math—all those things that are language-based activities. Struggling with learning language, using it flexibly, understanding the abstract nature of it, being able to hold information in your head, synthesize that information, carry it over to a new setting, pull it forward in an efficient manner, make connections between things—everything the kids do in academics is really a language-based activity."

Consider this an absolute for children with autism: Theory of Mind skills can be taught, and they must be taught.

When Bryce latched on to the Winnie the Pooh books and movies at around age seven, what tickled him especially was "Hoo-hoo-hoo HOO! That's what Tiggers do best!" Followed, of course, by Tigger messing up whatever the activity was and deciding that Pooh sticks, climbing trees, eating honey, etc., was not what Tiggers do best. I thought of Tigger's fumblings as I read through an excellent chart Christine put together for Bryce's teachers, illustrating "What Bryce is best at" and "What Bryce is challenged by," including suggestions for addressing those challenges in the classroom and at home. Recognizing our child's black-and-white core strengths and using them to push into the realm of the gray is what it's all about. Equally critical is recognizing that those strengths—things our Tiggers do best—can lull us and their teachers into assuming that they are automatically able to extend these skills to larger context. In hard fact, they cannot do that at all—until they are taught. To the uneducated, Eeyore tells us, an A is just three sticks. It's an apt metaphor for your concrete-thinking ASD child.

A huge factor of Christine's effectiveness as a speech language pathologist can be attributed to her devoted efforts to educate the educators, to interact with Bryce's teachers and with me in a manner that helped us understand those deep-seated Theory of Mind issues that are not apparent on the surface. I've adapted her work here in the hopes that you see your own child or student, and be able to take steps toward helping him conquer these critical skills.

Just because he can follow a schedule

Doesn't mean he can

- create a schedule
- easily assimilate random changes to that schedule (such as changing an assignment's due date due to illness or inclement weather)
- remember information that changes daily or weekly.

You can provide visual guidelines that help specify

- the task needing to be done
- the timeframe in which it needs to get done
- the steps needed to accomplish it.

How this plays out in real life for Bryce: Bryce's strength is that he is faultlessly punctual to the minute (we call him the Time Cop) and that he never, ever misses a homework assignment. He craves this kind of organization and, in middle school, achieving it involved his learning to use a calendar-style student planner to record assignment due dates, and having teachers provide project outlines with specific dates for each increment of the project to be completed (which should be mandatory for all assignments and all students, shouldn't it?). For all three years of middle school, Bryce chose Study Skills as one of his electives. It might not have been as much fun as art or drama, but he felt that having the extra support each day paid off in added confidence in his work, and less time spent on homework after school.

This strength/challenge carries over into literacy:

Just because he can

- follow a series of events presented in linear order

Doesn't mean he can

- follow a series of events presented out of order or out of familiar context.

You can

- verbally reinforce and review temporal aspects of the events and details of narratives or real-life situations
- provide visual supports or encourage child to create his own visual aids.

Just because he can

- recall facts in prompted situations such as cued oral discussion, multiple choice, matching lists or word bank tests

Doesn't mean he can

- retrieve knowledge in free-recall mode, such as assessments structured as story problems, or tasks involving multi-step directions.

You can

- provide prompted or cued assessments to compensate for impaired free recall abilities and slower processing speed
- employ alternative assessment methods, such as oral assessment or assessing work in a manner similar to how it was taught
- assess the quality of homework and class work vs. test or quiz outcomes.

How this plays out in real life for Bryce: A dramatic example of this occurred as I helped Bryce study for a geography test. The test was to be a blank map of the USA wherein the students would fill in the names of the fifty states. In free-recall mode, Bryce was able to come up with 30–50% of the state names. But when I gave him *the first letter only* of each state, his accuracy rose dramatically. The teacher agreed to test this way, and the result was that Bryce aced the test; this slightest of prompts pulled forth the full breadth of knowledge he had in his head. It's hard to say which of them, teacher or student, was more pleased.

Bryce's teachers also weigh the quality of his homework, his participation in classroom activities and his level of effort above the outcome of any particular test or assessment.

Just because he can

- remember concrete facts and details (rote memory)

Doesn't mean he can understand

- why those facts are relevant
- how those facts may be interrelated
- how they may apply to a larger or completely different context
- how they may suggest further facts (inference).

You can

- explain or demonstrate how facts and details contribute to "the big picture"
- provide supporting visuals
- provide opportunities to use new facts, concepts or vocabulary in new ways
- specifically identify passages containing inferential knowledge
- review and check for comprehension of figurative language, non-literal language.

Just because he can

- follow clear, concrete directions given directly to him

Doesn't mean he can

- understand expectations presented to the whole class or group, or that he can follow multi-step directions without visual support.

You can

- provide written and verbal prompts for necessary steps and outcomes
- check for comprehension at each step in the process.

How this plays out in real life for Bryce: There is a complicated brew here, and as teachers we walk a delicate line: we want to encourage his independent execution of work, but know that he is still working on knowing when to ask for help. Every day, groups and assignments shift, and the dynamic is ever-changing (which is, in fact, the definition of "dynamic"). We can't be complacent and assume that because he "got it" yesterday that he gets it today and from here out. Constant vigilance is the watchword—it may be unobtrusive, inconspicuous, but nevertheless, constant.

Just because he can

- complete work independently

Doesn't mean he can

- recognize when work needs revision
- work collaboratively with others to complete assignments or tasks.

You can

- provide cue cards or verbal prompts to check, reconsider and revise his work when necessary.
- in a group activity, provide structure for the activity and clarify each person's role within the group; team the ASD child only with flexible and supportive group partners.

- always check for comprehension.

Just because he can

- answer questions in a small group of familiar people

Doesn't mean he can

- retrieve information and volunteer answers quickly enough to keep pace with a larger group.

You can

- provide pause time for the child to formulate response
- assess group participation skills in small structured groups.

I've heard Tigger described as a "poster child for AD/HD" (attention deficit/hyperactivity disorder, a close cousin of autism spectrum disorders). It's true that Theory of Mind skills are not what dear Tigger does best, at least not yet. "I didn't really bounce Eeyore," he protests in a grand display of faulty social pragmatics. "I had a cough, and I happened to be behind Eeyore, and I said *'Grrrr-oppp-ptschschschz.'*"

What I think Tigger does best is maintain his zesty worldview, even when the chosen activity turns out to be more difficult or unpleasant than what he bargained for. He is always up for new experiences. This may be the most useful Theory of Mind skill of all, and perhaps it cannot be taught per se. Perhaps it comes naturally after we diligently teach "all of the above," and the net result is a child who experiences success and confidence.

The Other Side of the Desk

As transitions go, my son's transition to middle school had been smoother than any parent with an IEP in hand could hope for. It had been a very good year with very good teachers. But as the year wound down with alarming speed, the scheduling of the annual IEP meeting just wasn't happening. Repeated requests—at increasing decibel level—to resource teachers went unresolved amid scheduling problems, administrative issues, illnesses and other roadblocks. When we finally did meet, five days before the end of the school year, I told the excellent resource teacher only half-jokingly, "You're almost there. Only five more days and then you are done with me."

And this excellent teacher stopped in his tracks and looked at me with surprise. "Oh no," he said. "No. I have had some challenging parents this year, and you are not one of them."

At that, it was my turn to stop in my tracks. What, I wanted very much to know, constitutes a "challenging" parent? It was too intriguing a thought to leave on the table, so a few months later, we came back to it. His very thoughtfully painted portrait of a "challenging" parent led me to ask other special educators, teachers of students aged toddler to high school across several different school districts, the same question. And while each came from their own unique situation, the common threads in their thoughts were striking. A number of these common threads formed the basis for my book *Ten Things Your Student with Autism Wishes You Knew.* Here then is the view from the other side of the desk, the voice of your special education teacher.

Be team-oriented.

A combative attitude does not enhance our ability to make progress with your child. Our relationship should be an alliance, not an adversarial face-off. We are all here because of the child; he or she is our common interest, and it is important not to lose sight of that. It is not about me or you, or whether we like each other.

Give me the courtesy of a clean slate.

You may have had bad experiences with previous teachers or schools, but putting past conflicts or issues onto me, coming in with guns blazing before you even have a chance to get to know me or my program is counterproductive. "This is what has happened in the past and I expect the same from you" is looking for trouble where, possibly, none exists.

There is a difference between being assertive and being aggressive.

And there is a cost. Teachers appreciate the parent who is a knowledgeable, effective advocate for their child. Knowing what your rights are and knowing the facts on the ground, requesting services and accommodations firmly but respectfully is light years removed from being a fist-pounder.

We are not here for the money or the recognition. We are here because we love these kids. In an ideal world, I want to share with parents any inside perspective I have about "the system" and how it affects decisions made about their child. But if I sense in any way that a parent will use the information in a way that comes back on me or threatens my job, it is only natural that I will not share.

Undermining me undermines your child's learning.

Communicating to your child that everything that is going wrong is the school's fault undermines your child's ability to trust me, to comply with necessary classroom boundaries, and ultimately, to learn.

All children, even special needs children, need to assume some level of responsibility for their behavior and its consequences. We are sometimes faced with parents who say, "I cannot believe my child would do such a thing. It must be somebody else's fault. If you had been doing this, he wouldn't have been doing that." Sometimes that's the case. However, when a parent insists it is always the case, I need to gently suggest that a closer look be taken at what is actually going on.

Step back and listen as open-mindedly as possible when faced with information that makes your blood pressure rise. It's very common for children to exhibit a different set of behaviors at school than they do at home.

Having to be both teacher and case manager can put me in a very difficult position.

Especially in early childhood education, it often falls on the teacher/case manager to identify the fact that my particular classroom or program isn't the best fit for your child.

Please know that when I tell you we need to transition your child to a different setting, it isn't because I "don't like him." Hear me as objectively as possible when I tell you that he is struggling too hard in the current placement and would benefit from a different setting, that we need to modify the IFSP or IEP and find a better environment.

Don't assume I know everything about your child.

I may only have the prior year's academic information, and perhaps no personal information at all. Tell me anything you think is important for me to know about your child as a whole person. Be a resource for us, a bridge between programs. Share with us what has worked or not worked with your child in the past.

We cannot do everything for your child.

Your child is entitled by law to a free and appropriate education in the least restrictive setting. That is not equivalent to the *best possible* education. Think of it this way: You get the Chevy; you don't get the Cadillac. You get safe, reliable transportation but you don't get the CD player and the leather seats. It's a distinction many parents don't understand: that special education is intended to provide for adequate growth, not maximum possible growth.

Federal law mandates that we make sure that kids who have a disability are making adequate progress, as defined and measured yearly in their IEPs. The idea behind it is that without accommodation, they wouldn't make adequate progress in general education, and therefore would not be getting a free and appropriate public education.

Let's say you have a fifth grader who is reading at a second grade level. It happens; teachers commonly look at their classes and see a developmental range, so there are kids who end up in fourth or fifth grade reading several grade levels behind. So we set a goal, in a calendar year, for the child to make a year's growth, which is what his peers would make. But he is still behind, he is not catching up. In order for him to catch up, he would have to outpace his peers. Some kids do that, but it's very difficult and not realistic.

We have many commitments to multiple content areas. If we were to spend half the day on reading alone—sure, we could help the kid catch up. But that's not appropriate because we give up everything else. And so we always have that discussion every year in an IEP meeting. We have a certain amount of time. How do we set goals? How much time do we need to meet each goal? How much are we going to be able to accomplish given math, science, social studies, all of these other content areas required and from which kids benefit?

Your child is not my only student.

When I am meeting with you, when we are in a discussion and problem-solving mode—in that moment, your student is the only one I am concerned about. But back in my classroom, I have anywhere from a few to a few dozen other students in my caseload, and I have the scheduling restrictions that naturally come with that caseload. It simply is not possible for the needs of one child to dictate my entire day. Asking that of me is painful for both of us.

Early intervention works.

Here is an extension of a universal truth: The earlier the better—and the *better* the earlier the better. Catch things early, intervene well, and include your family, not just the school. No one was ever sorry they intervened early, but legions of families regret "waiting to see if he outgrows it."

See the positive in your child.

Have an honest understanding of what the range of your child's disability means, but also recognize his strengths. Too often, the most difficult parents to work with are the ones who cannot see the positive qualities of their kid. Their focus is stuck on what the child can't do. Perhaps they do not want to have a child with a disability. Perhaps they are stuck in the grieving process. But for the teacher, it is very hard to deal with.

Promote independence.

You were your child's first teacher, and you will still be his teacher long after he moves on from my classroom. Help your child learn to do things for himself, rather than doing them for him. Many teachers are parents themselves and understand the time-stress families face. But whether it's homework or personal organization, expedience in the moment will impede his learning to be independent in the long run. If you pack and unpack his backpack for him every day, how will he learn the importance of being organized, know where things are when they are needed, how to find items or information? The parents who are most effective are the ones who teach as well as parent. The two are synonymous. "The object of teaching a child," said nineteenth-century American writer Elbert Hubbard, "is to enable him to get along without his teacher."

The Wind Beneath My Wings

THIS IS A BE-CAREFUL-WHAT-YOU-WISH-FOR STORY. IT'S ABOUT THAT queasy feeling you get when it's time to walk the walk, to test that independence you've worked so hard to help your child achieve.

We were paddling in a new current that year. Bryce had started middle school in September. He left behind seven years at a school where staff knew him intimately and cared about him deeply. The middle school staff met us with all good intentions, but the warm welcome couldn't mask the irrefutable fact that we were starting from scratch with a team who had no familiarity with his learning needs, nor any emotional connection.

And there was an oversized shoe waiting to drop. It's name was Outdoor School, a widely cherished program in our county wherein all sixth graders go to local camps for a week to learn about native ecosystems. A terrific program, unless you have a child with autism and an auto-immune disorder requiring careful medication. Bryce was scheduled for the week of October 17th. My concerns were many. He had never spent five nights away from home without family. I would be placing him in the care of strangers: two teachers who had known him less than six weeks, and the rest of the camp staff, who knew him not at all. The routine he would be expected to follow would be completely unfamiliar; he'd be participating in an unadapted curriculum. He would sleep and eat with children he had never met before. Perhaps worst of all, he would be confronted with "camp food." With his severely limited palate, I could only picture (without too much hyperbole) his slow descent into starvation.

He didn't absolutely have to go, and both school and camp staff assured me they would make any accommodation necessary. Bryce himself wasn't sure he wanted to go, changing his mind from hour to hour, as he worried about the overwhelming unfamiliarity of the staff, the kids from other schools, the food, the living arrangements, the routine. And, he stated matter-of-factly, I need help. Will there be anyone to help me?

I met with his teachers. I talked to the camp nurse, did a meal-by-meal review with the head cook. I laid out all my concerns and they responded with the following accommodations:

- His resource teacher would go for the entire week.
- He would be assigned to an experienced cabin counselor (usually high school students), not a first-year staff person.
- He would have a supplemental paraeducator with his group for field study units.
- I would provide substitute meals for the ones that weren't acceptable to him.
- He would have the option of calling home if he needed to (not granted to other children).
- He had the option of leaving midweek if it simply wasn't working for him.

So I let him go. I had to let him go because I didn't have a compelling reason not to. I let him go because I had anticipated and supplied contingency measures for all the needs I could think of, and provided all the back-up possible to provide. I let him go because he went with the understanding that he wasn't stuck; he could bail out at any time. And I let him go because, after a decade of carefully orchestrating his life to ensure successful experiences, I felt the ground shifting under us. Neither he nor I would get through the rest of our lives without taking calculated risks, and yes, experiencing failure. It was time for a litmus test—for me every bit as much as for him.

I knew this because ringing in my head down through the years of his childhood were the astute words of his special-education preschool teacher: "I know you don't like putting a label on your child. But take the label, and take all the services you can get with it. You want him to be an independent adult."

You want him to be an independent adult.

I had to let him go because my gut was telling me that we had a better than 50-50 chance he would do okay. And perhaps the harder job was separating my own fears from his. I feared, to the point of nausea, hammer blows to his hard-won self-confidence. Would children not familiar with him consider him odd, a target for that special brand of thoughtless taunting at which children are so adept? Would he suffer those knife-to-the-heart moments that haunt every autism parent? Would he return depressed, deflated, and defeated? Even worse were my fears for his actual physical health, which were double-barreled: in the face of strange people, food, and outdoor substances, his challenged immune system could begin to slide dangerously, conceivably going unnoticed and unattended to. Compounding that, an ill-timed flare-up of his digestive disorder could have socially devastating effects.

Blessedly, I don't think he pondered those things. So those particular fears were mine alone, and they sat alongside my other, more selfish ones. *I* couldn't imagine five days without him. *I* would have trouble sleeping. So I spent the last two weeks before he left doing what I knew I was supposed to do, even though I did it knowing that I was convincing myself every bit as much as him. *You are ready for this,* I told him. *You are going to have a great time. You'll have all the back-up you need, you'll have familiar meals, your teacher will be there, and I'm only an hour away if you need me.*

He asked for a visual schedule of the daily routine and one of his meal set-up. We planned, cooked and froze his meals. We packed boots, toothbrush, pillow, flashlight, and photo of his kitty, Maria. He put together a small portfolio of his art activities for down time.

We both sported plastered-on smiles as he boarded the bus. *See you on Friday.* I continued to smile, smile, smile as the bus pulled away and his face in the window receded into a blur. In the car on the way home, the dam broke. "I don't think I can do this!" I sobbed to my husband. A few hours later, Bryce's big burly brother Connor showed up with tears in his eyes. "It's terrible without him," he lamented.

After dinner we sat by the fire, the 3:00 pm departure feeling like years ago, although it was still only 7:30 on Sunday night. It occurred to me that we were about to discover something we probably knew all along: that Bryce is the true soul of this family, our consciences and our aspirations, and without him we are ... well ... wasteoids. Sunday dragged into Monday and still I felt disemboweled.

On Tuesday I woke up to the unexpected salve that would get me through the week. Bryce had written me a note and his teacher had made his way to a computer to email it to me. "Outdoor School is half boring and half fun. I'm getting enough to eat. I made a friend today, she's a student leader named Starburst."

Things are going well, his teacher added. I'll give him any message you send back.

A large portion of my anguish evaporated in that moment. Bryce sounded so ... typical.

When he climbed off the bus three days later, he was undeniably different. An unmistakable aura of confidence preceded him down the steps.

"How was it?" I asked with shaking voice. The Million Dollar Question.

"It was great!" he answered. "I loved it."

I've never known quite what to do when life gives you more than you hoped for. I had only hoped for him to get through the week with a manageable amount of challenge. "I loved it" was a gift beyond anything I dared to imagine.

"He's always doing that to us," chuckled my mother when I told her. Again, as he has done so many times before, he has met the circumstances one measured step at a time and ultimately exceeded our expectations. "When do you think we will learn?"

That day I learned. I learned that George Eliot was right: those who trust us, educate us. Bryce was able to step away from lifelong safety into a new adventure because he trusted absolutely that I would not send him ill-equipped into a situation where he couldn't succeed. Because he trusted me, he could trust his own inner resources.

I learned that by giving a child roots, we also give him wings. In the giddy moments after his return, I confess to conveniently forgetting the weeks of preparation, disquietude, and doubt. I wondered—momentarily—how I ever considered not letting him go. At the same time I knew the value of that doubt: it had produced the actions that laid the groundwork for our success.

Next time Bryce sallies forth without me, neither of us will feel like we are stepping into an abyss. Next time we'll already have the playbook in hand.

The Song That Never Ends

THE EMAILS AND NOTICES FROM BRYCE'S MIDDLE SCHOOL TELL ME that Teacher Appreciation week is approaching again. And again, I will happily do my part. I will bake the cookies for the potluck luncheon, help my son write the poem for the scrapbook, contribute the handmade scarf to the gift pool, and whatever else the committee asks of me. I will do it because I very truly appreciate all that Bryce's teachers do for him.

But this year I will go beyond all that. I will reach back across all the decades of my adult life to the teacher I most appreciated. I never told him so, and now it's time. Between our own educations and those of our children, hundreds of teachers touch our lives. Some are here and gone with the wind, some will make us smile (or fume) years later, and a few will find a forever place in our hearts. Why? What fairy dust do these few possess above the others? In my case, it was a teacher barely older than I was myself whose subject matter, music, was but the framework for numerous unforgettable life lessons that have borne me along since.

Thirty years ago, I took three terms of Music History from a college instructor I remember only as Larry. Thirty years later, I can still say he was the best teacher I ever had. I've written volumes about teaching different learners, and much of what I believe came from him. He was a treasure.

My last year in college was spent in Larry's classroom, a bit by accident. During that senior year, I found myself in the fortunate position of having front-loaded all my degree requirements; I was free to spend my entire last year on electives. I worked at the local public radio station hosting a classical music show, so it seemed logical to opt for a three-term course in music history; it was "only" two credit hours. Not until the class was well underway did I realize that this was no fun little music-appreciation elective; it was a serious 400-level course populated entirely by music majors. I was horrified and traumatized, and after the first mid-term, took a drop slip to Larry's office.

"What is this?" he asked, voice full of curiosity as he poked the pink paper across his desk.

"It's a drop slip," I sighed, wondering why he was making me state the obvious. "I made a mistake. I didn't realize it was a 400-level class, and I'm in over my head. I am not a music major."

He leaned back in his chair. "So you are not enjoying my class?"

"Actually, I like your class a lot. I just can't keep up. I don't have the background."

The chair thumped forward. "Okay, you force me," he said. He smacked open his grade book and with delicate pencil tip, directed my attention to a line near the top of the page that had my name on it. "There are forty students in this class. You had the third-highest grade in the class on the mid-term."

He let it sink in a minute—how greatly I had misjudged myself—before continuing.

"This is a music history class, not a music theory class," he said gently. "You may even be at an advantage over the music majors because your head is not crammed with theory."

"But I feel so overwhelmed!" I protested. "You said we were going to discuss the differences between Haydn's music and Mozart's, and I cannot tell the difference!"

He leaned even further forward and let every word land like lead. "That's—because—I—haven't—taught—that—part—of—the—class—yet."

Another sinking-in moment passed. How unrealistic, my expectation that I would already know what had not yet been taught. Not only had I low-balled my own competence, I had iced it with a layer of unreasonable expectation.

"After I teach that part of the course, you will be able to tell the difference." Yet more sinking-in. Then, briskly: "So, no, I will not be able to sign that drop slip for you."

The little pink paper stayed in his office, at the bottom of the wastebasket, and I left with several profound lessons, none of which had anything to do with music. All that I would learn from this very young teacher was just beginning.

I continued on with Larry, enjoying both the class content and his rather non-standard teaching and motivational style. All assignments must be in on time, no exceptions! The penalty for missing a due date was fearsome: a mandatory trip to the listening lab to sit through the full-length version of *Parsifal,* a five-hour Wagner opera. While the dread of this penalty was palpable, the class nonetheless was wildly admiring of Larry's ingenuity. There was much discussion of whether he "meant it," but no one was willing to take that chance.

Larry taught with more energy than of the rest my professors combined. How many teachers out there could inject wonder and excitement into a Gregorian chant? He had the utter gift of being able to convince his students that what he was teaching was important for them to know. Time and again, he would stop cold in mid-sentence, either whirling around from the blackboard or leaning forward palms-down on whatever desk was handy, and clarify for us: "This is important! You need to know this!" His tone precluded disagreement. We all caught his contagious enthusiasm and we did want to know! And that was some trick when it got to be spring term with a class full of seniors, but he never let up. I've thought about it frequently through the years as I've watched so many of my kids' classes just coast for the last few weeks until the end of the year. The cumulative loss of learning opportunity never fails to make me sad. It was yet another Larry lesson: don't slow down just because the end is in sight. Finish strong!

It's possible that I was primed to learn through Larry's positive examples because I had already gotten a glimpse of the reverse as well. I changed majors the day the chair of the Department of Education refused my request to waive a class requirement I felt I had already fulfilled. He barked, "What makes you think you are different from everyone else?"

At first I thought I had heard him wrong. I was training to be a teacher, the most basic tenet of which was supposed to be: acknowledge that each individual student is unique. And here was the head teacher telling me that the teaching-teachers-to-teach curriculum was set in stone, and how dare I question that? Learning through a different path or at a different pace was not acceptable. *What makes you think you are different from everyone else?* I should have put the turd back in his pocket with, what makes you think I am the same as everyone else? But I did not waste one single more word on that man or his department. Fifteen minutes later, my advisor stamped her feet in frustration that the field of education might be losing a potential asset, but she couldn't change my mind.

A window closes, a door opens. Dr. Department Head was a bad teacher, but he did me a favor. He drove me into journalism, a career I never regretted for an instant. But most importantly, he raised my radar to what would become a critical issue in my life. Lack of respect or allowance for different learning paths was something I would need to confront again and again when my different-learner children came along. And with them, of course, I could not simply walk away.

But I digress. I'm not done with Larry yet. We are in the second quarter, and yes, I did learn to tell the difference between Haydn and Mozart; learned quite easily, thank you kindly. But I couldn't know that disaster was waiting on the morning of the final exam.

It's barely light when I arrive for the test. I've already been up several hours studying. I'm well-rested, everything is fresh in my mind, we are go for launch.

Three essay questions form the exam. Two of them I know cold. "I could write a book!" I think, and do. But the pen sputters to a standstill on the third one.

I have no idea what the question is about.

I don't recognize the term I'm being asked to define. Am sure I have never seen these words on a page before. Have no recollection of a class discussion containing these words. Sit and stare at the vast, blank answer space; wonder if even the polar tundra is this vast and blank. I am so blank, I cannot even *fake* an answer to this question. I do some math. With no possible answer for what amounts to one-third of the exam, my best possible grade is a D, maybe a C if Larry takes pity on me and judges the other two sections flawless. There goes my hard-won, odd-woman-out success story, swirling down the toilet of sonata-concerto form. The exam period ends and I turn in my paper, two erudite answers alongside the vast, blank polar tundra.

It's only a matter of time until I am summoned back to Larry's office, standing meekly in front of the same desk where I had presented my drop slip a few months before. Of course I know why he has summoned me, and for the occasion I am wearing my best I-told-you-so face.

My exam sits on his desk, the blank space stares back at me once again. As before, he pokes curiously at my paper. "WHAT," he booms, "is THIS? *What is this*?"

"It's my exam," I sighed as if on rewind, wondering yet again why he was making me state the obvious. "I am sorry, but I wracked and wracked my brain and simply do not know the answer to that question. Don't you think I would have written something—anything—if I could have? I am *so blank*. I do not know the answer."

"Huh." He's looking at me, and I just know his mother must have told him a hundred times not to lean so far back in his chair. "You don't remember our discussions on _____?" And he recounted several lessons that I did in fact remember quite well.

"Yes, I do remember that," I told him. "But that's not what this question is asking."

"Oh." He seemed thoughtful. "Well, tell me what you do remember."

So I did; I talked and talked. Rather knowledgably, I thought. At the end of my discourse, he said: "That's what this question was asking. I was pretty sure you knew it."

"That's it?" Oh, *no*.

"That's it." He smiled broadly. "You got hung up on one little piece of terminology. Funny how that can happen sometimes, huh?" Then he did the extraordinary Larry thing that seared him into my memorable-teacher banks forever. He leaned forward and marked a big A on the top of my paper.

"I just want to know that you know the material. That's all that matters to me," he said.

That's all that matters to me. All that mattered to him was that learning had imprinted. What was not important to him was my inability to prove it in a narrowly prescribed way. He was so slick about clearing a different pathway for me to express what I knew that I didn't even see it until it was over. Not ten minutes after skulking into his office in shame, I left feeling empowered, energized and eager to go on.

Larry was all of about twenty-six years old, nowhere near a full professor, but he was the best teacher I ever had. The most important thing he did for me was refuse to let me quit. Even though I was in an environment where I was the odd duck out, he believed I would succeed, expected it of me, gave me the tools to do it, accepted no less—and so succeed I did. From him I learned how to reframe and meet challenges, and I experienced the power of having someone flat out believe in you even when you don't believe in yourself. I learned that that we can't know something we haven't been taught yet, and that real teaching is not about imparting facts but about inspiring the student to love not just the subject matter but the learning itself. And I learned that there is far more than one path to retrieving learned knowledge.

In time I learned what some of Larry's teaching peers thought of his offbeat style. One of my profs raised his eyebrow—just a bit—as I sat telling him how much I loved Larry's classes. "Isn't he a bit of a three-dollar bill?" he asked.

What a rude, sour grapes remark, I thought. But I was only twenty years old and not yet versed in telling my elders, "What a rude, sour grapes remark!" I no longer think Larry's style was offbeat. I think he was in sync, and the others were off-rhythm. It wasn't unlike the moments that occurred so often throughout Bryce's childhood, when it would strike me that his concrete view of the world, so devoid of spin and BS, was right, and the rest of the world would be better off doing it his way.

As the years went by and I wallowed deeper and deeper into the world of my children's public educations, it became clear to me that there was far too much distance between the conventional one-dollar and five-dollar bills. What if your child requires some denomination in between? What we really need is more three-dollar thinking, especially at the high school level.

As an ADHD student who was able to hold his grades just above a 3.0, Connor's high school performance was considered by most teachers and staff to be "good enough." Several of the more outstanding teachers did push him to excel, but many had no curiosity at all about his learning style, and a few were downright hostile to the suggestion that his learning needs might require more than just an admonition to "try harder" or "pay attention." His grades were always a teeter-totter of As in project work and class participation, brought down by the cement boots of Ds on quizzes and tests. Although there was a clear record of uneven learning ability, he didn't qualify for an IEP or a 504 and he didn't qualify for talented-and-gifted; he was somewhere in that immense faceless pool in the middle of "good enough" students. I was left to work through endless individual situations with individual teachers. Time and time again I would ask, can we modify the assessment method to more accurately determine what he actually knows? A few were willing to accommodate, but too frequently came the standard, amiable answer, "Sure! We can give him more time on the tests."

More time on the tests. As if this is the only thing that might be wrong with an assessment method. What I learned in Larry's classroom twenty-five years earlier was that allowing *eternity* for a test won't make a difference if what is needed is a different avenue of information retrieval. Something as simple as, in my case, rephrasing or reframing the question can prompt a flood of recall.

In Bryce's case, too. We had a sterling example of this in his eighth grade social studies class. His teacher, Dave, had a stated goal for Bryce: "I just want him to learn as much as possible." Dave was willing to be very flexible in assessing him. While studying for a geography test, I noticed that Bryce's free recall of the facts was in the 30–50% range. (Free recall is a notoriously weak skill in many students with autism spectrum disorders.) But when I gave him the slightest prompt—the first letter only of the answer—his recall was dramatically higher. Dave agreed to test this way because, he said, "I really want to know what he knows."

Bryce aced that test. I have no doubt that because of this and many other instances that accumulated throughout the year, Dave will be one of Bryce's Larrys. He will be remembered as the kind of teacher who was willing to seek a different inroad, a path less traveled, so that a child who learns differently can still find relevance in a wide array of subject matter, and experience both the excitement of discovery and the thrill of being successful in a manner consistent with who he is. He asks and answers the question: what is more important: creating a person comfortable with and welcoming of lifelong learning, or a person who knows how to upchuck information in order to pass a one-size-fits-all test?

So wouldn't it be interesting if teachers were required to present the same question three different ways? What might we discover about the manner in which individual children learn, retrieve, and express? What might we discover about whether and how teachers, as Larry did, inspire students to want to learn, to enjoy learning as a means to knowing something relevant and interesting, with no angst about whether it will "be on the test."

It's been more than a few years since I decided that I'd broken my kneecaps for the last time falling before the test gods, whether classroom or government-mandated. One memorable day I confronted a group of Bryce's middle school teachers with a standardized test and asked, what exactly does my child get out of this? They acknowledged that the test was formulated in a manner that disadvantaged him, one frustrated special educator going so far as to say that it "played into every weakness my students have." So, *what exactly does my child get out of this?* The best we can say, they said, is that he gets the experience of taking a test, because tests don't go away.

Before I could even take a breath to reply, one of the teachers jumped in with, "Are you trying to get us to tell you that these tests are no good?" And in the millisecond that I was weighing a diplomatic answer, she continued, "Because I'll say it."

"You'll say it?"

"Yes, I'll say it."

This very young and courageous teacher was not even born yet on the day Larry told me that knowing that I had *learned* was all that mattered to him. She and those like her give me hope that the time is coming when those who revere testing over learning will get off the stage and let the Larrys of the world have their day. Maybe then we will be allowed to mine the infinite buying power of a three-dollar bill.

Sometime after I wrote this essay, I thrummed my head for the better part of a day, called the university alumni office, dug out old yearbooks, until I finally came up with Larry's last name. Google found him in two seconds flat. He is still teaching, more than 20,000 students later, albeit not at the school where we met. And finally, finally I was able to tell him thanks—for never letting me give up.

We exchanged long emails, during which I told him (amid many things) that I never did listen to a single bar of Parsifal. After he read this essay, he commented, "You really should try Parsifal .... Remember, we need to grow beyond our biases."

He is still *teaching me.*

The pebble hits the pond, and we can never truly know the extent of the ripple effect we have upon others. I'm still learning, but I know that the effect is infinite. When it leaves us, and especially when it comes back to us, it can be a journey of pure joy and affirmation.

Postcards from the Homefront

Home. A single place, a thousand faces. We escape to it, and we cannot escape from it. Safe haven and combat zone, and everything in between. Home is where life with autism is most real. It is where we nurture the skills of hand, head and soul needed for a very different three Rs—Real life, Real love, Real character. *Cultivate.*

If You Never Start

"If you never start, you'll never have to worry about stopping." That's my parents, talking to the teenaged me about smoking.

"If you never start, you'll never have to worry about stopping." That's Dr. Springer, my kids' first pediatrician, talking to me about spanking. "Once you start, where do you stop?" he adds ominously.

"If you never start, you'll never have to worry about stopping." That's me, endlessly explaining to people why I never go to Starbucks.

You can see that this adage is at work in my life. But it's not always a conscious choice. Sometimes it is intuitive. It is the reason we never had Nintendo®, Game Boy®, PlayStation® or any other video game system in our home. I had no actual list in my head of reasons why we shouldn't let our boys indulge in this very common contemporary pastime. I just let inertia do its job—we didn't have one and if we never got one we could just bypass all the fights about which games were okay, how much time they could spend on it, was it interfering with homework, and of course the expense of the never-ending demand for new games and upgraded equipment. To be honest, raising two boys with non-standard needs constantly taxed my stamina to the outer limits and "one less thing on the plate" was frequently an appealing option.

Some years later Dr. Springer had retired and we were getting to know a new doctor. He really got my attention with his reaction to an offhand comment I made about not having any video games in the house.

"That is probably the single most important parenting decision you ever made for these kids."

I didn't know him well enough then to know if hyperbole was his style or if this statement was sincere in its incredible weightiness. The most important parenting decision I ever made? More important than moving to a new home to get them into better schools? More important than not allowing smoking in our home? At the time, I ended up merely accepting it as a nice compliment. But over the years my mind would wander back to it: "... most important parenting decision you ever made *for these kids*."

Seven years down the line, it finally occurred to me to ask him what exactly he meant, especially the qualifier, "for these kids." Did he in fact even remember saying it to me?

I can well believe I said that, came the answer. And I would stand by it. And here is why: **Video games—all video games, not just the violent ones—magnify the issues of autism and ADHD.**

In that one sentence, he made me see video games in all their unvarnished glory: immersive, addictive, over-stimulating, socially isolating, sedentary, non-productive, unrealistic language vacuums that frequently reinforce and reward socially unacceptable behavior.

Those are all ugly, compelling arguments against video games, but the bottom line is much more subtle, even insidious, and it is this: No parent or teacher, says my doctor, can compete with the sheer pace of a video game. Real life simply does not and cannot move that quickly, reward that quickly, wipe-out-and-start-over that quickly. The artificial expectation it sets up for the child is insurmountable. It's never enough. By contrast, life in real time, at the speed of real life, is boring. The child, already over-stimulated, seeks even more stimulation. The child who is already hyper becomes yet more hyper.

"Don't never generalize!" my family jokes, and of course I cannot tar all video games with the same brush. There are worthwhile ones out there. But if your child has autism, it's sobering to confront just how actively video games can work against the very challenges we are trying to surmount. Consider:

Limited, Unbalanced Sensory Involvement

Video games overstimulate the visual and auditory senses, while offering no involvement or development of the other five senses. The drum-like repetitive action and artificial sound encourages perseveration. Jana Cahill, an adult with autism, tells me "video games are not what they used to be," that the action has become "too real, too bright and too fast." The games have gotten ever more intense and that "being an autistic, the graphics give me a headache until I get used to the games."

And Cahill disagrees with the argument justifying video games as being good for hand-eye coordination. "I don't believe that video games improve hand eye coordination," says Cahill. "If it's bad to begin with, it only gets worse."

There are about a jillion activities that develop hand-eye coordination much more constructively: drawing, puzzles, blocks, Legos, dressing dolls, digging dirt, Nerf sports, kitchen pursuits. These activities can be just as engrossing as video games. When my kids were little, they would beg to play "water cups." They entertained themselves for as much as three hours at a time with a trickle of water from the sink or outdoor hose. They would pour it back and forth between all sorts of containers, mix it with whatever was close by (dirt, paper napkins, leaves), sing, add shaving cream or food coloring, get their clothes and hair wet to see how it felt. Visiting cousins and friends were just as intrigued, although one was incredulous: "My mother would never let me do this—I'd get dirty!" I put her in a swimsuit, assured her that she was 100% washable and that she would leave as clean as she came—it would be our dirt-y little secret. Once she got started, I literally could not tear her away, even when Dad showed up.

Inactivity

"Get up offa that thing!" shouts James Brown's thirty-year-old song. You can't turn your head and sneeze anymore without confronting alarming information about obesity and other organic diseases that are escalating sharply in today's children who aren't active enough. But there's more: a growing body of evidence that suggests cognitive learning is directly related to physical activity. Schools that incorporate physical activity programs see positive effects that include increased concentration, improved math, reading and writing scores and fewer disruptive behaviors. In my own life, I was astonished to see Bryce make marked leaps in reading, math and general cognition immediately after learning to swim, and later, to ride a bike. I am 200% convinced of this link, but I also know that finding physical outlets that our ASD kids can wholeheartedly enjoy can take more searching, planning and facilitating that it does for NT kids. For now, start thinking about non-team sports and non-competitive active pursuits.*

* Fifty such activities are listed in "To Activity and Beyond!" at the end of Chapter One of my book *1001 Great Ideas for Teaching and Raising Children with Autism Spectrum Disorders*. "Easy Adaptations for Aspiring Athletes" in Chapter Six offers ways to modify common sports skills, rules and equipment to facilitate learning for kids with ASDs. Many school districts employ adapted PE teachers as part of their special education motor team; such specialists can be invaluable in helping children develop the skills that will enable them to participate successfully with their peers in PE and other physical activities.

Obscures the Line Between Fantasy and Reality

Distinguishing between fantasy and reality requires the ability to engage in perspective-taking, something children with autism are notoriously lacking. For many of our kids, that inability has ominous implications as applied to Ninja-chopping, motorcycle-crashing, machine gun-blasting video games—or any other "harmless" fantasy portrayal. Do you dare imagine what Wyle E. Coyote *really* looked like after he went over that cliff with a cache of dynamite?

Bryce had a class assignment one year wherein each student wrote and presented a short speech in character as a famous ancient Greek. Bryce chose Alexander the Great ("the only name on the list I could pronounce," he said, only half-joking). His classmate Michael (also on the spectrum) chose Zeus. When I commented that Zeus was a mythical person as opposed to Alexander who was quite real, Bryce's startled reaction was: "What? Does Michael know this?" I met up with Michael's mother at school shortly thereafter and relayed the question to her. Her reaction: eyes rolling a bit sadly as she replied, "Does Michael *ever* know the difference between fantasy and real?"

It's something to consider if your child suffers from nightmares—and can't quite tell you why. Temple Grandin has stated frequently that she avoids movies with graphic depictions of violence because, as a visual thinker, the images sear permanently into her brain and she cannot get rid of them.

Rewards Unacceptable, Illegal Behavior

Nor is it realistic to expect the child with autism to understand that the violent or destructive action in a video game is "for entertainment purposes only." This is the part I find most scary. Games whose object is to blow up, blow away or lop body parts off of opponents *reward successful violent behavior.* The child receives instant positive reinforcement for killing and maiming. Worse, as opposed to TV, he is participating in the violent activity rather than merely watching it. Worst case scenario: these are behaviors that, if emulated, can later land him in jail. The nuances of law enforcement are going to be enough of a challenge for him without the added handicap of pondering helplessly why it was okay in his favorite game but not okay on the actual corner of 5th and Elm.

Social Skills Void

Think of all the elements that go into healthy social development. Ask yourself if video games fulfill any of these for your child: engaging in positive interpersonal interactions, building a sense of worth and self-definition, expressing himself through creative thinking and activities, being a meaningful participant in a group. Are video games helping him learn to impose the self-discipline needed to structure his time, set reasonable limits, prioritize tasks? Are they helping him learn to distinguish and choose gracefully between wanna-do's and hafta-do's? Or between privileges and rights?

Language-Development Black Hole

Language development is among the most urgent of issues for many, many children with autism, and in this regard, there are few worse friends than the video game. Played in isolation, there is no useful language happening at all. Even in parallel play with a friend or sibling, attention is fixated on the screen and whatever minimal verbal exchange that takes place generally relates only to what is happening on the screen.

A Role in Regression?

Does your child demonstrate social or cognitive regression following summers and extended school breaks? If he's whiling that time away in front of a screen, it might be useful to question the role of video games. All skill development, whether it's reading, making conversation, taking turns at games, hitting a tennis ball, baking brownies, or tracking down the evil Super Mario double, takes practice. Extended time off from school shouldn't be time to abandon social and cognitive learning. Do the math: a child who is in school 6.5 hours a day, 175 days a year is spending only 22% of his 16 waking hours/365 days in that school. For the other 78% of his time, the instruction is up to you.

And as a parent, there is no way to escape or bypass making an investment of your time in whatever video game system you decide to allow into your home. Do you yourself understand the system itself and the games well enough to bail your child out when he doesn't "get it" and his frustration starts to boil over? Will you allow only educational or strategy games and not competition games which set up a winner/loser scenario; are you willing to preview all games? One of the first games we were ever exposed to was a supposedly educational timed math game. The child would choose from multiple-choice answers while the clock ticked away. If the choice was incorrect, the game would honk and blare: "Brrrr-aaa-ppppp! You're a *loser*!" Admittedly, this was many years ago and games have come a long way since then. But so have the cheap-buck artists. If you do not preview the material to which your child will be exposed, you simply will not know. Many children with learning differences struggle with low self-esteem. Some of this struggle comes from their limited ability to place things in perspective: there is Winner and there is Loser and there is nothing in between. It isn't only a game; it is a test of self-worth! Will you be able to veto and circumvent inappropriate games in the face of relentless resistance? "[That's] something you don't see on the news: a parent returning a[n inappropriate] game that their underage kid bought," says Cahill. "My parents were the only parents I knew of who actually bought and played the video games I chose."

A child's job is to explore the world. For our kids with autism, that exploration may be a little more tenuous, a little more treacherous. But explore they must and that means touching, talking, tasting and trekking, *discovering*. For all time before the twentieth century, this happened without the aid of a video screen. Long before my doctor had anything to say about it, the great writer Johann Wolfgang von Goethe did: "Talent develops in solitude, character in the full current of human life."

The Power of a Cookie

IT WASN'T THE FIRST OR THE LAST TIME I RECEIVED SUCH A CALL AT work. Four-year-old Connor had committed some crime against one of his fellow day care inmates, and "it would be a good idea" if I came and picked him up early. Mothers who get these calls experience many emotions. But rare is the mother, no matter how patient and understanding, who can take those calls without an occasional twinge of exasperation. Exasperation comes in two flavors: sometimes for the child, sometimes for the teacher.

That day my exasperation was mixed with "not-again" weariness. So imagine my surprise when I was greeted with an agitated but upbeat child who wanted to know if we could go home and make cookies. Certainly not, I started to say. Why would I reward your prickly behavior? But before I could utter a word, the teacher took me aside. Say yes to the cookies, she said.

He's had the preschool equivalent of a tough day at the office, she continued. You won't always be able to fix his problems with a cookie. My daughters are in their twenties now, and I can't fix their problems with a cookie. You can't know how I miss those days. Don't pass up the opportunity while you have it.

I didn't have Bryce yet, and had no inkling of autism or even the ADHD caller that was soon to greet us with all the force and warmth of a freight train. But even knowing nothing about neuro-pediatric disorders, it began to dawn on me that day: it was counter-intuitive that the fault in a two-way interaction gone wrong between preschoolers could always be absolute, and always be my child's.

We did go home and haul out the cookie sheets. In between adding the oatmeal and the chocolate chips, my son told me that he knew he shouldn't have bopped Jacob but he just got tired of how this classmate knew just how to needle him when the teachers weren't looking, then cry victim when he succeeded in provoking. Had I not agreed to the cookies, I might never have learned this and been able to advocate effectively on behalf of my child.

Cookies are social communication therapy; they have that kind of power. Over the years I sent cookies to Little League games, teacher appreciation buffets, birthday parties; they magically opened the door to the social conversations that were so difficult for my children to initiate and sustain. I smile as I remember back to the few years when the end of my father's career and the beginning of mine overlapped. We both worked downtown and would meet with our brown bags in the park. The inevitable panhandlers would happen by, asking if we had any spare change. Dad was always politely apologetic, saying, "I don't have any money on me but would you like a cookie?" Out came the baggie of vanilla sandwich cookies. These men nearly always lit up with genuine smiles and said, "Well gosh, thanks!" They liked the cookies but even more, liked the kindness. The language of cookies is always a language of kindness. Who ever heard of a mean-spirited cookie?

But the ultimate power of a cookie lies on the other side of the world, where my Marine corporal niece bore witness to horrific things happening in a place called Fallujah, Iraq. Please tell me what

I can send, I begged her. Candy, magazines, sunglasses, toiletries? Nope. All she wants is photos of the family—and cookies. She wants cookies. When I protest the three-week delivery time ("They'll be hockey pucks!"), she assures me they will be okay. Just put 'em in plastic bags and send 'em, she says firmly.

Three weeks later, a cheerful email declares, "The cookies were delicious! Eating them in one sitting wasn't planned but I had a lot of help. Thank you to the 10th power!"

Just like that long-ago advice, she's in her twenties now and I certainly can't solve her problems with a cookie. But I hear her saying it can still make a meaningful dent.

Lcpl. Frankia Bernstein completed her tour of duty and received a combat ribbon for her service in Fallujah. The cookies from home, she says, were part of what "gave me a reason to keep on going out there."

Connor is approaching twenty and my guess is that he too will defy conventional wisdom. There will still be days when Mom's chocolate chip cookies can soften life's blows, even if just a little.

Uncommon Gifts for Uncommon Kids

SEPTEMBER 1997. THERE HE SAT, TICKLE ME ELMO, IN ALL HIS FUZZY red glory atop the store display. Only $7.99; could it be? It's less than nine months since stampeding parents had literally trampled each other in quest of this rarified muppet. But yes, it was Elmo all right, with giggle and all other parts in good working order. And the store was Goodwill—stalwart recycler of fickle desires, a harsh mirror reflecting how very fleeting childhood loyalties are. "He probably has rabies," remarked nine-year-old Connor.

How grateful I was in that moment for what being the parent of a child with autism has spared me. Never a Nintendo®. Power Rangers were powerless over him. No Pokemon®, Furby, Game Boy® or Lion King for Bryce. As a youngster, he never watched TV, thereby bypassing all the frantic media attempts to brand him from birth. Unbelievable as it may seem, he simply wasn't interested in typical toy store fodder.

I will say that it made gift-giving challenging. The Toys "R" Us® catalog held no sway in our house; my favorite catalog was Southpaw—a company whose specialty is sensory integration developmental products, fun stuff like swings, inflatables, fine-motor games and toys. As autism awareness has increased over the past decade, more and more sensory-friendly toys are available, but back in those olden days, I was largely on my own.

Over time, I became an unwitting expert in unconventional gifts. I learned that resourcefulness is priceless. And I learned that, without a wish list or even words, kids do tell us what they like, if we just listen and watch.

Martha Beck's son, the title subject of her book *Expecting Adam,* is my role model for really cool gifting. Martha relates a Christmas morning tableau of listening to her daughters grouse that their gifts weren't exactly what they wanted. Adam, a child with Down Syndrome, began opening a package containing an extremely noisy toy from an otherwise thoughtful friend who had included an eight-pack of D batteries to power the toy. Adam opened the pack of batteries first. Before Martha could say, "That's not the real present," Adam, his face reflecting "astonished ecstasy," raced through the house identifying every wonderful thing that ran on batteries. Appliances, toys, tools. "He babbled excitedly about all the things he could do with this fabulous, fabulous gift," Martha recounts in the book. "It began to occur to all of us 'normal' people in the family that batteries really were a pretty darn good Christmas present. They didn't look like much on the face of it, but think what they could do! Put them in place and inanimate objects suddenly came to life, moving, talking, lighting up the room. Something about Adam always manages to see straight past the outward ordinariness of a thing to any magic it may hold inside."

Adam is right. Many fun, meaningful and uncommon gifts never saw the inside of a toy store or an electronics aisle. They come without screens and keypads, and they don't beep or talk back. Some of the earliest writing I did about autism was about the gift-giving creativity I was forced into by my non-conformist son. As problems go, it was not one to complain about.

Southpaw was my favorite catalog because sensory integration is never far from the forefront of living with autism. When my Southpaw money ran out, I made the happy discovery that perfectly ordinary items, when presented in unusual quantities or unusual presentations, made for gifts that delighted my kids, started new family traditions, and never, ever ended up in the Goodwill bag. Multiple cans of shaving cream, bushel baskets of marker pens, a whole bucket of flashlights, cookies packed in toolboxes, and "pirate treasure" second-hand jewelry actually buried in the backyard in a trunk.

We made the kids active participants in both ends of the gift-giving equation. First, they had to work for their loot. If you wanted the birthday candy, you had to help Mom make the grocery-bag piñata for the party (our favorites: the octopus and the vampire), and then you and your guests had to smack the daylights out of it. At holiday time, we carried on a ritual started by my father: the annual treasure hunt. When the kids are young, the clues were just simple drawings. As they learned to read, words were added. They got older ... and still they wanted the treasure hunt. They got smarter ... and the clues had to increase in complexity, with rhyme and pun and inference (but not too much!) to where they started to challenge me as the creator! Even in their teens, my boys were still rabid for the annual hunt and didn't really care what was at the end of it, as long as it was chocolate. The tradition had become the gift, much more so than any transitory item that passed through their hands at the end of the chase. I have little trouble imagining that they will delight their own children with these hand-me-down customs.

And we encouraged them to give others the gift of themselves, whether it was their own artwork framed (more on this in a minute), a photo snow globe, a toy or game meant to be played together with the recipient. It truly is more blessed to give than to receive, but choosing meaningful gifts for loved ones is not a skill we are born with. Witness the malls filled with migraine-suffering procrastinators on December 24th each year. Now, take three giant steps back and view it as a child with autism, already struggling to understand empathy and interpret the feelings of others. "What do you think Dad would like?" is a question so broad it's bound to induce high anxiety rather than creative thought.

But resist the urge to simply buy something and slap a "from Jimmy" gift tag on it. Gift giving is about learning to consider the feelings and preferences of others, and for our children, it is one of those elusive Theory of Mind skills that will not come without long, loving and gentle repetition and reinforcement. So start now by having them participate, with your guidance, in choosing or creating those gifts of self that are guaranteed to please. Seeing expressions of pleasure and receiving heartfelt thanks for their efforts will eventually establish the cycle of reciprocity so important to our social nature.

Your own gift-giving can support this gift of self. Gifts that enhance a child's self-esteem are not only priceless, but usually right at hand. Many's the family that proudly displays their child's artwork on the refrigerator. Taking the extra step of having their work professionally framed says, you are mighty special. All through their childhoods, nearly every gift-giving occasion in our family included at least one professionally framed piece of our children's art. Our house has become a veritable museum of their work over the years and nothing underlines their efforts more than a constant stream of visitors' attention. It also helped me realize that the art you have in your home is very personal and contributes every day to your child's sense of comfort and security in his surroundings. My husband and I have very different taste in art, but we were solidly united in our admiration of our children's output. As their handsomely framed work overtook the walls, it filled our home with the aura of its distinctiveness. Each piece became a friend, complete with the wonderful memories and history that make friends such a valuable part of our lives.

When my kids hit their teens, they did reach a point where they enjoyed some of the more typical gifts like music CDs, DVDs and movie-logo T-shirts. But the die was irretrievably cast. Having bypassed Nintendo, Game Boy, Play Station, Power Rangers and Hulk, there was no lapsing into such things. Resourcefulness is still the hallmark of our holidays.

One year I ducked into a fabric store about a week before Christmas to pick up an extra skein of yarn. "So," asked the young clerk, making conversation. "Have you been to the mall this week?"

"No," I answered, digging for change. "I don't do malls."

"Ever?" She sounded incredulous. "Or just at holiday time?"

"Ever," I said. "I haven't been in a mall in years."

"Wow," she breathed. "*Where do you buy things*?"

So here I am, back at the same chuckle with which I started this chapter. No mall, no catalog, no disappointed pouts, no financial hangover. Now *that's* merry and bright.

The Gift of an Experience, Experiencing a Gift

IN THE PROCESS OF CREATING THIS BOOK, MY EDITORIAL DIRECTOR read the foregoing essay and commented, "My favorite gifts are tickets or passes to special events. Giving someone an experience can be profound, especially if it is an opportunity to spend time with that person."

Her remark triggered a flood of recollections for me. Bryce was like many children with ASDs in that giving him the gift of an experience was, oftentimes, indeed profound. Profoundly difficult. As a young child, his life experiences—the range of things he was both willing and able to experience—were distinctly limited. His teachers constantly urged me to expose him to a broader variety of experiences. While I was never in disagreement with them in theory, taking a child with so many sensory challenges (and the behavioral fallout thereof) out into a big wide world that involved tickets, elevated levels of noise and crowds packed into tight dark quarters was, plain and simple, more easily said than done. The same was true of Connor with his exuberant but impulsive hyperactive personality and behavior. Over the years, we tried Sesame Street shows, the circus, children's theater, sports events, concerts, all with the same result: premature exit. Needless to say, we avoided airline travel, where premature exit simply wasn't an option.

As with gifting, I believe children tell you when they are or are not ready for particular experiences. The message may not come in words. One memorable preschool year, Bryce's class was singing adorably on stage at the holiday program, he on the end of the row sporting a smile so static it bordered on scary. Then, without a twitch of a facial muscle disturbing that smile, he began side-stepping towards the wings. Three inches at a time. Smiling, smiling. Three inches, three inches. Three more inches. When he had side-stepped to within a few feet of a safe exit, he broke for it. I stood up. He rushed for me, and his smile beamed brighter with each step. And no, I did not feel all eyes on my back as we continued out the door, especially after I told off the charming grandparent behind me complaining, "Would sumbuddy get that big kid outta the way?" I was proud of that big kid. He wasn't ready for the experience of stage performance; at the hoary age of three, he already recognized his need for sensory self-regulation, did not yet have the language to tell us so, and his exit was mature beyond his years. A principal later told me it isn't uncommon for the occasional "typical" preschooler to rush from the stage in tears. At that time, the idea of autism had not yet entered our lives, but I was starting to get an inkling that my son was not typical. As the years went on, I recalled this incident with ever-increasing pride in how he had handled himself, and by the way, what's with expecting "typical" three-year-olds to perform on stage? A video of a similar performance of Connor's class at the same age features a noticeable number of the group standing mutely with fingers glued to the insides of their noses. This is not the sort of image they thank you for when they grow up. (Unless you are the class comedian, who took the opportunity to announce, "I'm digging for ants!")

So the type of broadening experiences that involved the purchase of a ticket were beyond the realm of the realistic for our kids for many years. My husband and I continued to enjoy these things as a couple, none more so than our holiday tradition of attending *The Nutcracker.*

I took ballet class for years, in childhood, in college, and as an adult up until I had children. When I met my husband, he had never been to the ballet. He was game to try it, though, and surprised me by becoming an adequate armchair critic in a very short period of time: "The triple pirouette was weak. Would have looked fine as a double." We went to *The Nutcracker* our first year together, and in each of the twenty-five years that followed.

The Nutcracker not only became our tradition, but gave life to traditions-within-traditions. One year we sat in front of two girls of eight or so, decked out resplendently in holiday taffeta and velvet bows. They whispered excitedly to each other throughout: "Oh! I know what those are! Those are snowflakes!" "Dancing mushrooms!" "Toy soldiers!" This delighted commentary continued until they became momentarily stymied by the *Waltz of the Flowers*. "What are those?" asked one. "I know what those are," announced the other after only the slightest hesitation. "Those are the Venus fairies!"

We managed, but only barely, to stifle our laughter. And every year since then, to the opening notes of the *Waltz of the Flowers,* we turned to each other and said, here come the Venus fairies!

When our niece grew old enough, we took her too. But that was only after she no longer made astute but inappropriate editorial remarks. To wit:

She was the first baby of her generation in our family, and I could scarcely endure the wait for her to pull herself upright so that I could buy her a toddler-sized tutu for her first birthday. With diaper bulging and bagel crumbs, not sequins, strewn across the stiff skirt, no prima ballerina was ever lovelier. At age three her mother took her to the dress rehearsal for a production of *Swan Lake*. All was well until the scene in which the prince and his hunting party come across the swan princess and her flock; he dismisses his companions so that he can investigate alone. Announced my niece to anyone within hearing: "He had to send them away because he could see that those are not real swans, only ladies dressed up like swans!"

Knowing this was the possible behavior of a well-mannered "typical" child, I wasn't tempted to chance it with my boys. If I felt a twinge of wistfulness sitting next to OPBs (other people's boys) with their holiday bow ties and hair combed handsomely back, I stifled it. My boys were lovable, enjoyable company and, of course, more handsome than any OPB. It's just that they were not inclined to sit still for anything longer than a Skittles commercial.

So I was taken aback when Connor came home from his second grade class one day and announced that he wanted to go to *The Nutcracker*. A dancer from Oregon Ballet Theatre had visited the school and provided an introduction to the story of *The Nutcracker* and to ballet in general. And what was the hook? "It has a Rat King and a fight scene!" I didn't know it then but this dancer, barely out of childhood herself, had taught me a lesson in how to introduce the new and different to a child who clings for dear life to the familiar and the predictable: go in through the back door of what interests them, however narrow the passageway.

I explained to him that a live ballet performance was not like a movie or a ball game. The tickets were expensive and it required sitting quietly for an hour at a time, without snacking, yakking or running to the loo. He insisted he could do it. I bought tickets on an aisle three rows from the back, ideal for the speedy exit, stage left, if necessary.

As the performance unfolded, I was visited by worry of an unforeseen variety. He was quiet, all right. He sat motionless, a seven-year-old statue complete with glassy eyes. Oh well, I thought, maybe he'll make it through the first act; then we'll cut our losses and head out.

The first-act curtain descended on the shimmering blue snowflakes, applause swelled and died. And still he sat. "Well?" I finally ventured. "What do you think?"

When Houston has liftoff, they get months of preparation and a second-by-second countdown. I got no warning whatever. He shot straight in the air, two feet of daylight appearing between the seat and his bottom. "THIS IS THE GREATEST THING THAT'S EVER HAPPENED TO ME!" he shrieked. We rushed to the lobby to buy the Rat King T-shirt (and the requisite brownie). Afterward, the ride home was a non-stop litany of everything about *The Nutcracker* that was grand and dazzling, followed by piteous wailing about having to wait a "whole 'nother year!" to see it again. In the years that followed, Connor settled into the tradition as comfortably as we had nearly two decades earlier.

And one long- and patiently-awaited year, Bryce let us know that the time was finally right for him to join us. The motivation was not a Rat King, or a brownie, or any other obscure detail of the experience. He was, he said, simply tired of watching the three of us go without him. I watched him out of the corner of my eye throughout the first act. Like his brother all those years earlier, he was inscrutable. And when the curtain fell? He didn't even want the brownie at intermission. He wanted to buy tickets for a second night. Do I need to tell you that we did just that? In the lobby before the show, he posed for a photo with the sugar plum fairy and a toy solider. Today, that photo still sits on a teenager's bookshelf, in its rightful place among the DVDs, sports trophies and Harry Potter books.

Our boys knew intuitively when it was time for them to join us for our annual outing. If that time had never come, that would have been okay too, but what I love most about my boys' zest for the ballet was the way they made space for it in their lives, right alongside the baseballs, trains, dinosaurs and poop jokes. It was real live holiday magic, truly a magnificent example of a successful "broadening experience."

Courtesy of the Venus fairies.

A Cool Pool Story

"If it be not now, yet it will come;
the readiness is all."

Hamlet

Once upon a time there was a boy named Bryce, a July baby born under the Water Sign, who nevertheless resisted swim lessons for many years. Then one summer—when he was ready and not a minute sooner—he floored us all by transforming himself from pool barnacle to swim champ in mere weeks, at the same time teaching us a lesson in grace and timing.

He spent the first three weeks of lessons telling his teacher that he didn't want to get his hair wet. Then the dam broke and it was like punching some internal fast-forward button. By the end of the summer he was swimming front crawl up and down the twenty-five-yard length of the pool, going off the diving boards, learning back stroke and breaststroke. In just five weeks, he had churned through five levels of the Park Bureau's swim program.

The following summer he joins his brother Connor's swim team. Approaching his very first race, no one has any idea what Bryce's reaction will be. Family and coaches stand in suspense. The starter blares and there he goes. He is swimming with complete aplomb, smiling—smiling!—the whole way and charming everyone poolside by waving to Mom and Dad as he goes by. His coach is left to shake her head. "Never saw a child *smile* when they swim," she chuckles. He finishes third and comes home with a ribbon, the first of many.

At the end of the summer, Bryce is assigned to the breaststroke leg of a medley relay team for the big citywide meet. Over five hundred swimmers participate in a two-day event that involves interminable waiting in a relentlessly raucous jumble of bodies and smells. The spectators cram in cheek by jowl, accompanied by enough lawn chairs, coolers, camcorders and sunscreen to open a small Wal-Mart. It should be a sensory hell for Bryce but he seems unfazed. He isn't a particularly fast swimmer, although he is never last. He doesn't trouble himself with the concept of competition. Get in the pool at one end, swim to the other.

Now he is taking his place for the second leg of the medley relay. The starting horn honks and the backstrokers launch themselves down the lanes. They touch at the opposite end and the breaststrokers take off. Who is that kid in Lane 6? He is flying. He is *flying*. His coach is dumbstruck. His mother is speechless. It's Bryce, of course. You can tell even with the cap and the goggles because he is smiling as he swims.

When the standings are posted, something impressive and unforeseen is right there in black and white: Bryce's team has finished in the trophies. He will be up front shaking his coach's hand at the awards dinner that night. I never dared to imagine such a thing. But obviously Bryce did. He actually made a second trip to the podium that night, to accept the team's Most Improved Award. "At this rate," said his teacher, "I'll see you at the 2004 Olympics!"

To this day, I am not exactly sure of the formula that took Bryce from the figurative "zero to sixty in three seconds"; how he tolerated and overcame such sensory-toxic surroundings will forever be something of a mystery to me. Five hundred years ago, Shakespeare's

Hamlet asserted that "the readiness is all." It may not be a lot more complicated than that. Bryce was nearly eight years old when the readiness arrived. The sensory intrusions of the pool environment were numerous and ugly; my efforts to remove as many obstacles as I could were a piece of that readiness, yes, but not the largest piece. Many parents, myself included, consider swimming an essential life skill, and waiting until my child was ready at age eight was just excruciating. But the exhilaration and the accomplishment at the end of that wait was proof certain of what our psychologist had told us in the beginning—he will unfold in his own time.

In the end the most significant accommodation of all was attitudinal: that it's not as much about flutter kicking and an overhand stroke as it as about allowing the child to explore his parameters without forcing expectations. "Acknowledge and respect that there is a fear factor for any child," our teacher said. "When a child is learning to swim, what is most important is the patience and the encouragement of both teacher and parent, allowing the child the freedom and the permission to progress at whatever individual pace makes them feel safe."

Bryce's triumph in the pool at the city meet thrilled me to the marrow—I actually had to leave the pool deck to compose myself—but it wasn't the start of something big. He took a very matter-of-fact been-there, done-that attitude towards swim team, and by the next summer, he made it known that he was moving on to a new frontier. A brave and beautiful amphibian, he left the pool for the siren call of the community theater stage. But that's a story for another day.

For all the years my kids were in swim lessons or swim team, many a session ended with a just-for-fun activity, and many times it was a game of Sharks and Minnows. It's basically a game of water tag. Someone is designated as the Shark and waits in the middle of the pool. The rest of the swimmers are the Minnows, who must swim from one end of the pool to the other without being tagged by the

Shark(s). Each swimmer who is tagged becomes a Shark for the next round. So, as the game progresses, it morphs from a game of tag to an obstacle course, as the Sharks begin to outnumber the Minnows and the odds of success for the Minnows shrink to nothing.

Across the wide spectrum that is autism, there will be those children who take to the water like fish, metaphor intended. For others it will be a figurative game of Sharks and Minnows. Many "typical" children must work to overcome a natural fear of the water in order to become swimmers, but for the child with autism, the issues are magnified. They are Minnows who must make it past the Shark-infested waters of innumerable sensory challenges, with plenty of social communication lampreys and piranhas thrown in. Small wonder plenty of our little Minnows never get past the (smelly, cold, slippery) locker room.

There is no end of sensory insults in the typical swim-lesson environment. Layer on top of that the fear factor and the pressure of expectation. Any one of these issues can render swimming lessons dead on arrival for your child. In our fish tale, I felt that my job—identifying and removing as many of those obstacles as I could—was the easier one.

Our adapted PE teacher advised us to first consider the teaching venue, because there are pros and cons to each.

Halt! Who Goes There?

Before you even get to the pool, do you have to traverse a cavernous locker room booby-trapped with clammy puddles, funky odors and screaming hair dryers? That alone will be enough to stop some kids. On top of that are safety issues, particularly if you are a mom with a boy or a dad with a girl.

Stranger-danger is real and scary enough for neurotypical children, but for your child with autism the thought is just heart-stopping. The outside entrance to most pool locker rooms is not visible from the pool deck. You must do whatever is necessary to keep your child safe in loose public venues like this. Some pools now offer family changing rooms, a boon for parents with opposite gender children If your pool doesn't, and you truly can't take your opposite sex child through the locker room (I did, without apology), ask if you can come in to the pool through a side exit, employee entrance, or other alternative where you can accompany him.

Okay, we made it out of the locker room; now we confront the actual hole with the water in it!

Indoor vs. Outdoor Instruction

Indoor pool sensory problems may include heavy chlorine odor, steamy atmosphere, echo-chamber effect of shouted instructions and continual splash, competing noise from simultaneous activities. One busy summer, we were contending with the noise of an adjacent class, the swim team practice, the steady *fwap!* from the springboard diving class, and the boombox music from the synchronized swim group at the far end of the pool. Outdoor pools pose sensory challenges of their own: water too cold or too murky/slimy (from dozens of kids slathered in sunscreen, peeing in the pool), floating dead bugs, weather issues such as breeze on wet skin, air temperature too cold, the occasional rain shower, visual and aural distractions such as people constantly moving around the pool deck, deck chairs being dragged, glare from the sun, puddles of melted snow cones.

All things considered, we opted for the indoor pool and went on to consider the mechanics of the actual lesson. The typical group lesson of six offered by our Park Bureau would not provide Bryce adequate personal space around him during the lesson or the kind of adapted communication he needed. We opted for semi-private lessons, which proved ideal. Bryce learned with two friends (far higher comfort level than a group of strangers), and the teachers incorporated fun activities like diving for rings, or inner tube "races." (Note: if you are considering private lessons, be aware that one-on-one instruction may be too intense for some children, causing them to feel the pressure of expectation or solo performance.)

Now Hear This!—Or Not

We asked the pool manager which times of day were the most and least popular and chose our lesson time accordingly. We asked our instructor to speak directly to our children from a distance of no more than two feet, to give clear instructions in plain language, no slang. We knew we had the right instructor when, from our perch in the bleachers, we couldn't hear a word she was saying to the kids. We didn't need to. Her written evaluation at the end of that first session said it all.

Wow! An eager swimmer and an absolute pleasure to teach.
Ear to the water, bubbles down, great job!

—

It Really Isn't About the Bike

BRYCE IS FLYING DOWN THE PATH ON A BLUE BIKE NAMED TERRY. The wind he's creating plasters his Jimmy Neutron t-shirt to his chest. His legs are churning with the ease and confidence of Lance Armstrong. And the best part is: he is indistinguishable from every other nine-year-old pedaling the path at the resort where we vacation every summer with my brother's family.

And, like Lance, it's not about the bike. As with so many other milestones in Bryce's life, I didn't fully grasp that until several years later. In his typical atypical way, he had taken the process and turned it inside out to suit him. I learned not that seeing is believing, but rather the reverse: believing is seeing.

Sarah is another indispensable person our school system sent us. She is an adapted PE teacher. We were at the beginning of kindergarten, and this was (yet another) service about which I knew less than nothing. What on earth is adapted PE?

"Not many people are aware of what we do and how it affects kids," she told me. Adapted PE specialists travel between several schools during the day, seeing a wide variety of physically and mentally challenged students, "although I personally don't feel that autism fits either of those categories," she added intriguingly. APE teachers provide modifications to PE activities and equipment so kids with challenges are able to participate with their peers. The motor team of which Sarah is a member was one of the first in the nation to serve kids.

During his two kindergarten years, Bryce attended a self-contained adapted PE class and participated in PE with the general education class as well. In the beginning, the IEP goals are simple: Hopping on one foot ten times and bouncing/catching a ball. Oh yes, and one goal not related to motor skills: "Bryce will resist imitating inappropriate behaviors." When I came to volunteer in the class, I saw him peeling off after a classmate who was continually making for the door. He did this time after time, cackling with glee. He clearly didn't get it. I discovered, with interest, that this behavior didn't occur in the general education PE class he attended in the afternoon.

Sure enough, by the end of first grade, adapted PE takes place in the general education setting, and, with appropriate peer models, the behavior issue has disappeared. Sarah writes that Bryce is able to participate in general education PE with minimal adaptations. She acts in a consulting capacity to the general ed PE teacher, advising him that Bryce needs both verbal and visual directions and is best placed third or fourth in line in order to motor plan for the activity.

By the time Bryce starts third grade, Sarah's involvement has decreased to a once-monthly observation and consultation with the teacher. During the fall quarter immediately following his learning to swim, her IEP progress record reports, "Bryce has amazed us all with his increased abilities. He is engaging more with peers and shows comparable skill levels in many areas. He shows more self-confidence and motivation, and really enjoys PE." With her encouragement and some research, we found a Little League spring baseball team that seemed suited to his lack of experience in the sport. In very short order, we found that he had no trouble batting, throwing or catching. In this same time frame, he learned to swim and experienced success on a summer swim team.

But the one thing that still eluded him was riding a two-wheel bike. In looking around his circle of acquaintances on the autism spectrum, it was a common denominator—none was riding a two-wheel bike. At age nine, he was growing too old for training wheels, adaptive trikes, alley cats, or other alternatives that would similarly make him stand out in the bike crowd in an undesirable way. But it seemed he could not manage to part ways with the stability provided by those training wheels, even though he had a powerful motivation to do so.

Connor was barely out of infancy and Bryce was but a twinkle in the future when our family began vacationing at Sunriver every summer with my brother's family. The original Gang of Four was nineteen-month-old Connor, my seven-year-old niece, and my two- and four-year-old nephews. Sunriver, a woodsy resort in the central Oregon high desert country, offered numerous appealing family activities from swimming to canoeing to horseback riding. But most appealing at the time, and remaining so down through the years, was the thirty miles of paved, flat bike paths winding their way through the landscape. The first few years, our bikes were a tangle of child-carriers and their requisite belts and straps. In each successive year, a sort of parallel history of our kids' childhoods unfurled between the spokes revolving through hundreds of miles of pine-needle encrusted asphalt, and the occasional unfortunate snake who didn't slither out of the way fast enough. Now when I look at those bike paths, I see the progression of our children, each transitioning from baby carrier to Big Wheel to training wheels to two-wheeler and finally, can we bike to the ice cream store by ourselves? I see what are surely authentic dents in the roadway where each of them took their most impressive spills.

Except Bryce, stalled at the starting line. He'll never take an impressive spill because he won't allow himself the opportunity. The pride of self and the thrill of two-wheeling isn't worth the risk and the fear of hitting the pavement in a heap of axle grease, lava dust, and blood.

He took to a tricycle with great enthusiasm at age two. Rode the two-wheeler with training wheels effortlessly at age four. Stopped, inexplicably, at age five. After that, would ride only with the odd combination of bike helmet and life preserver, the kind that fits around the neck. It was a mighty unusual sight, and even though none of his relatives ever breathed a single syllable that betrayed its peculiarity, he soon simply stopped riding at all. Two years of concerted effort on my part accomplished nothing.

It was during one of Sarah's occasional-consult calls that I lamented my ineptitude. He had achieved so much, it seemed unlikely that he simply wasn't able to ride a bike. The failure had to be not in his ability, but in my teaching.

"I will teach him," Sarah announced. "I will do it on my lunch hour."

I should not have been amazed that she was willing to go that far. I desperately wanted to accept her offer, so my protest was feeble and it crumbled at once under her adamance. He would bring his bike to school, it would stay locked in the gym's equipment room when not in use. She would work with him once a week in the gym during lunch recess. Bryce agreed to all of this with little hesitation—thank you, PE gods!

To make a short story shorter, Sarah taught Bryce to ride a bike in less than forty-five minutes—three fifteen-minute sessions. During the first session, she accomplished what I couldn't manage in two years—got him to agree to take off the training wheels. During the second session, she brought a balance bar to work with him. Afterward, she called me and said, this is going to take a little longer than I originally thought. The balance issues are greater than I anticipated. Please be patient, we will get there.

That's okay, I said. Just try to let me know when you think he's close because I'd like to see him ride for the first time and possibly camcord it.

Deal, she said.

During the third session, she called me in a whisper: "Ellen, I'm so sorry." My first thought: he's hurt. My second thought: he's crawling along in the gym, how hurt could he be? Before I can vocalize either of these thoughts, she continued, "He's riding his bike. I'm watching him. He's going around and around and around the gym. I know you wanted to be here but I just had no idea he would do it this soon."

So I went to school that afternoon to retrieve son and bike; he tore around the playground, bumps and all, as if it had never been any other way. It seemed like magic but of course it wasn't. What's behind a lot of magic is actually logic, careful planning and consummate patience. Here's what happened in that enchanted forty-five minutes.

1. Sarah led up to the actual sessions during the lunch hour. She and Bryce talked about what would be best, getting him involved in every aspect of learning to ride the bike. He chose the time and place—it could have been done after school, Sarah could have come to our house, he could have done it in the gym or out on the playground. He chose—he wanted to have his own bike, his own helmet; he wanted to be in the gym, he wanted it to just be Sarah and him. "All of these factors were really important," says Sarah, "because he made the choice. It wasn't forced on him; it wasn't somebody else saying, this is what you need to do."
2. Sarah was able to recognize and play to his motivations. Sunriver was the biggest one. "It was about being part of the family. For many years leading up, he was a spectator, not a participator." But the spectating was not wasted activity. Intricate motor planning was in process. He was able to watch, hear and motor plan what the other kids were doing in order apply it to himself and decide how he would do it. He was further motivated by the school setting. The training wheels came off in a flash because he didn't want anyone at school to see him riding with training wheels.

3. At the first session, Sarah had Bryce show her how he rode his bike, knowing that he wasn't yet able to actually ride the bike. She knew that he knew how to get up on the bike and that he knew about trying to balance the bike. She was unremittingly encouraging, telling him that if he fell, just get up and do it again. Get up and do it again. "I made no negative comments. I verbally reinforced each piece of what he had already meticulously motor-planned: 'good steering, Bryce,' 'nice wide arms on the handlebars, nice pedaling, nice balancing.'" She also had him tell her when it was okay to be in his space, to touch him, to hold his bike, to offer support for him so that he could maintain his balance. "It wasn't me instructing him on how I as a teacher would learn how to ride a bike. It was Bryce instructing me how to instruct Bryce how to ride the bike."

> **What is motor planning?**
>
> Motor planning describes the action formulated in the mind before attempting to perform it, sequencing a skilled activity from beginning to end. It is an ability that grows out of the sensory integration development process. Many children with autism become quite good at it. Because of his motor planning skills, "I really believe Bryce 'knew' how to ride a bike before I taught him how to ride a bike," says Sarah.

4. During the second session, Bryce asked Sarah not to hold the back of the seat. Yet he never fell because he innately knew when to put his feet down. "Walking the bike" is common for many children. But Sarah had detected a balance problem and had brought along a piece of adaptive equipment called a balance bar.

A balance bar is a simple pole or broom handle placed across the handlebars of the bike. The child holds on to the balance bar without holding on to the handlebars, to get the feeling of the balance on the bike. Sarah held the bar and walked with Bryce as he was pedaling and sitting, so that he could get a feeling of where his center was, where his balance was on the bike. Then she slowly brought the bar down to the handlebars.

Being in that upright position is a very unbalanced situation for a child. "Remember when you were a kid riding your bike without your hands on the handlebars? That was unbalanced. What I did with Bryce was to start in his most unbalanced position first and then took him to the easier position second. Kind of backwards."

And the third session is history. "It just all came together for him," Sarah says modestly.

It was close to three years later before I thought to ask Sarah if Bryce's learning experience was typical for a child with autism. She said she didn't know, because Bryce was the only child with autism she had every taught to ride a bike. I found this incredible.

She insisted it was about belief, not motor skills. "You believed that Bryce could do it," she says. "And you instilled that belief in Bryce. Bryce wanted to do it for himself, but he also wanted to do it for you. Not all parents have that faith in their child, the belief that he or she has the ability do things than they can do, and the child feels that."

And coupled with belief, the critical component of being able to let go of ego and timetables. Maybe I "should" have been able to teach him to ride a bike myself—I had taught Connor on a "normal" timetable—but I had reached the point where accepting outside help was the only scenario that made sense. My failure would not be in my lack of success in teaching him to ride a bike, it would be in neglecting to look outside myself for the resources to achieve our goal.

It takes courage and initiative, says Sarah, to be able to say, "I think my child can do this, but obviously I am not the one to teach him. I may not be teaching him the way that he needs to be taught." Bryce learned because every subconscious expectation had been removed. Alone in the gym with Sarah, he was away from the prying eyes of neighborhood children who might snicker at his training wheels, away from a parent who had successfully taught an older sibling at a much younger age. He was away from the specter of the other bikes in the garage poised for the annual vacation, away from having to worry about "being brave" if he fell. "Be aware of how much information kids get about themselves from the outside world," Sarah told me. Children are exposed to expectation all around them, from seeing the six-year-old who is riding without training wheels, to knowing that the family vacation is only four weeks away. "Part of being a parent who is aware is being open to that. And having open communication with a child with autism is often difficult because feelings, emotions, and conversation in general are difficult for them. To be able to recognize, empathize, identify the feelings of others is something that needs to start with the parent."

I Sound Like My Mother—I Hope!

IT SOUNDS CRAZY, BUT I TRAINED FOR THE MARATHON OF RAISING A child with autism.

I didn't do it on purpose, of course. I did in the course of playing the cards I drew. And that hand came with a wild card, who was also my King of Hearts: Connor, a child with textbook attention deficit/hyperactivity disorder. Emphasis "hyperactive." He dragged me on the roller coaster ride of my life, but when a sidecar called autism pulled up beside us, I realized that ADHD had been a walk in the park, a training run, for all that lay ahead of us as we stepped onto the spectrum. Hard to imagine being grateful for such experience, but I was—immensely.

A child with undiagnosed, untreated ADHD can be a taxing proposition for even the best of preschool teachers juggling an entire class full of four-year-old needs. Despite an excellent teacher, pre-K was rough for Connor. But as he came into his kindergarten year, we were fortunate enough to land both the right doctor and the right teacher. The doctor, a developmental pediatrician, told him: "You are a fast, powerful, shiny black locomotive—with no brakes. We are going to get you some brakes. Remember that having no brakes doesn't mean that train is a bad train—it simply doesn't have the right parts, and we are going to get you those parts."

The teacher's concern was more global. She felt that he has been beaten down by the relentless cycle of adults and even peers trying to corral his no-brakes behavior. "You'd better take them just as they come to you or you will not make it in this job!" was her stated philosophy, and she was a twenty-three-year veteran of taking them as they came. Even so, and even as Connor perplexed and challenged her, she cared about him deeply and ultimately steered us to the course that we followed into grade school and beyond. It began with her telling us: "This year is about my re-building his self-esteem. I do not care about his academics—clearly, he is bright and that will come. What he needs most is to go into first grade feeling good about himself."

Her lesson, that self-esteem had every bit as much to do with achievement as did "brains," was top of mind when it came time to face down the challenges of Bryce's autism. I weighed the impact of nearly every word I said to him, and considered how it would be heard by him. It wasn't at all easy to do this in the heat of confrontational or despairing moments. But oh, how worth-it it was. No child comes through youth completely unscathed by the biting or thoughtless remarks of their peers. But Bryce's inordinately high level of self-confidence has made it possible for him to weather unkindnesses with reactions such as: "Well, kids who think they know everything don't know that they don't," and "They are immature and still learning," and the Advice for All Time, "I just don't listen." More on this in a minute.

Having poured copious effort into attempting to flame-proof my kids against the sticks and stones of words that could hurt them, I was greatly appalled when, one cozy winter day, I was browsing through a well-known parenting magazine and came across a terribly unfunny essay entitled *I Sound Like My Mother*. "Remember all those annoying phrases you promised you'd never repeat to your child? How many did you say today?" this article brayed. The infamous list starts off with "Because I said so, that's why," moves on to "Stop crying before I give you something to really cry about," drones away and finishes big with "Do as I say, not as I do." There was more, much more, but I think you get the picture.

I realized that I myself could never repeat those phrases because my mother never uttered one of them. Neither have I, and it's not because my children have never danced on my third nerve. They are, in fact, the Fred Astaires of that. It's more that I simply couldn't bring myself to speak to the people I loved best in so mean and disrespectful a manner. "This hurts me more than it hurts you." Then what's the point?

I showed the article to my mother to get her reaction. She barely deigned to offer one. "These are clichés," she said. "Do people really say these things?"

Apparently, I replied.

"Why would anyone say these things to their children? I never needed to."

That's not quite true. She never chose to. My brothers and I were thoroughly typical children and she certainly could have found reason to say these things had she wanted to.

That is not to say that my mother didn't spout doozies of her own that have indeed popped out of my own mouth unexpectedly. "Don't stick your elbow out too far, or it may go home in another car." "If you eat too much watermelon you will turn into one." These are, of course, things you should never, ever say to a child with autism lest the visual association he creates keep him awake and screaming for weeks.

But my mother espoused her own brand of wisdom, and as it turns out, it is just right—and then some—for raising, respecting, and nurturing a child with autism. Not only am I grateful as a daughter for her example to me, but even more grateful that my neuro-*atypical* children have her steady presence and life-celebrating attitude as they grow up. I know she is not the only grandmother who has brought the gifts of patient insight and a wellspring of compassionate concern to her grandchild with autism. My mail frequently bears provocative messages from grandmothers of children with autism. Their questions are sometimes anguished but almost always the right ones. They are startlingly clear-eyed, free of denial; they are non-judgmental, and always, love for their grandchild shines through, as does their pride in what the child has already accomplished against such odds. I find myself wondering if they subscribe to the same special brand of perspective on life as my mother, the same recurring pearls of wisdom for which I am most grateful:

"Life is too short to be little."

This powerful statement is attributed to English Prime Minister Benjamin Disraeli. My grandmother espoused it at every turn and my mother carried on that tradition. French novelist Andre Maurois elaborated on it: "Often we allow ourselves to be upset by small things that we should despise and forget. Here we are on this earth, with only a few more decades to live, and we lose many irreplaceable hours brooding over grievances that, in a year's time, will be forgotten by us and by everybody. No, let us devote our lives to worthwhile actions and feelings, to great thoughts, real affections, and enduring undertakings. For life *is* too short to be little."

Disraeli won't mind if I take this sentiment one step further: Life is too short to (fill in the blank). Life is too short to grieve for what you don't have rather than celebrating what you do have. Life is too short to spend time wishing you could undo or relive the past, or to refuse to explore the future for fear afraid of what it might bring. Because ...

"It's best not to dwell on the might-have-beens."

The poet John Greenleaf Whittier embodied this philosophy with his famous line, "For all sad words of tongue and pen, the saddest are these: 'It might have been.'" The twin exercises of this philosophy, as practiced religiously by my mother, are counting your blessings and keeping your focus forward-looking. It works. I am so much happier and better able to cope with life's curve balls when I remember to do this. It's quite magical how it squeezes bitterness and regret right out of your consciousness.

"We do the best we can with what we've got."

This Teddy Roosevelt gem is a wonderful, graceful way of saying we never shirk or make excuses for what we need to do. But we also know when to cut ourselves some slack and we know where to back off those infernal perfectionist standards we sometimes impose on ourselves. "Courage doesn't always roar," states my favorite mantra by Mary Anne Radmacher-Hershey. "Sometimes courage is that small voice at the end of the day saying, 'I will try again tomorrow.'"

"It's better to have it and not need it than to need it and not have it."

Mom said this a lot, whether it was to take along a sweater to the evening ball game or an extra swimsuit on the vacation. As a kid, I simply hated hearing it; I usually didn't want to make the effort to take along the "it," but she was so inarguably right.

And it is a superb mission-control strategy for traversing life's terrain with a child with autism. Getting into the habit of contingency planning for Situations A, B, C, D and E has saved me and my child untold amounts of stress and time lost to damage control. If it meant we lugged more gear, traveled with stopwatch precision and thought in patterns of nonstop what-ifs, at least we seldom didn't have It when we needed It.

"You have two ears. Let it go in one and out the other."

This great piece of advice for dealing with cranks, grouches, teases, loudmouths, dolts and other irritants came directly from Mom's father, who had the revered reputation among family and friends as being a peacemaker. I won't say it's easy, but it's sage counsel for those detestable moments when some ignorant, unmannerly stranger (or relative) sees fit to let you know how poorly they judge your ability to deal with your distraught, disintegrating, sensory-overloaded child. Zingy retorts and dirty looks are okay with me if you have a ready arsenal of them. I admit I once held up three fingers and told a very nosy lady to "read between the lines." But I like more the serenity you get from knowing, really knowing, that you are doing the best that can be done with your child at that moment, and that you and you alone are the one to make that determination.

And when I feel my fists ball up, at least figuratively, in stifled desire to flatten the kid who calls my son stupid or weird, I have to take my cue from him, to again marvel at his above-it-all response: "I know I'm not stupid. I just don't listen." And I am forced to wonder if the ability to do this hereditary.

"If God intended women to camp, He would have equipped them with the same gadgetry he gave men."

Okay, I had throw this one in and, yes, my mother was raised a city girl. This woman hiked North America with my father from Denali to New Mexico to Nova Scotia but when the sun sank low, any camping to be done was Hilton-style. Dad had a thirty-seven-year career in the Army and the US Forest Service, spending many summers in remote enclaves of the National Forests of the Pacific Northwest. He loved being in the woods, but he knew that in marrying my mother, he was getting a gal with a finite outdoor comfort zone. He considered it was an acceptable compromise for the pleasure of her company and they had many wonderful outdoor experiences, just none that involved tents and sleeping bags. Looking back, it was a great lesson for me in gracefully accommodating a beloved child whose preferences were distinctly limited. For many of our early years with Bryce, he mightily preferred his own bed to any other sleeping arrangements, and that limited our family travel. But in time he became much more of an adventurer than I. I'm my mother's daughter. Each summer I stay home to write while my boys all go camping together.

I can only imagine what my children will say in years hence when they reflect on what their mother sounded like. But truly, I did the best I could with what I had! And if ever anyone flips me the epithet, "You sound like your mother," you can be sure my response will be, "I hope so!" Oh, I do hope so.

Postcards from the Heart

THE HEART IS YOUR STEADFAST TRAVEL COMPANION, THE NAVIGATOR OF your road less traveled. It leans into the curves with you, accelerates into the straightaways. It slows for the potholes, and yes, it must stop periodically to refuel. But seldom—seldom—does it lead you awry. *Listen.*

What We Leave Unsaid

"The truth is rarely pure and never simple."

Oscar Wilde

It was an innocent question posed to me in an interview: "I'd like to ask about the optimistic tone in your books ... whether you've at all sugarcoated your delivery of information."

This puzzled me. Had the reporter missed the descriptions of our early years in autism, the ferocious meltdowns, the social isolation, the school confrontations, the bone-weariness both emotional and physical? But deeper than that—why would I? Of what real help would it be to real families like yours to put the rose-colored shades on our experiences?

Anyone who chooses to write their family story is opening the door to allow strangers a very personal and potentially painful look at their lives. Believe me, it requires soul-searching. Before I began to write about my family, I had to question my motives. I had to decide how much I would share and how it would affect the people I love most. I wondered: would there still be any value in sharing what was left after I declined to share that which was too personal and painful?

I have always told you the whole truth, although not necessarily the God-awful truth when I judged it would dishearten the reader, or would actually hurt the person about whom I was writing. That's an equation whose answer is a moving target. I want to share Bryce's trials and triumphs in a manner that is positive but realistic. What I don't want to do is share in a manner that will one day make him hate me. Interesting it is that amid all the cyclones of emotion that have ripped through our home over the years, the one phrase that has never passed the lips of either of my children is "I hate you!" Somehow my children knew those words would have simply trashed me. Perhaps they intuited that my love and determination for them underwrote whatever the overwrought situation of the moment might be. They respected that vulnerability in me, and I could do no less for them.

So, I am thankful that Bryce never smeared feces or ate glitter, but if he had, I would not have written about it. It's so easy to write about our kids now, with chat groups and blogs. This easy sharing of information can do powerful good, but I squirm when I see parents exchanging stories that will spark fury and distrust in their children ten years from now when they pop up in some internet archive. Even as I write this, I am deleting an anecdote that you would have found highly entertaining. But Bryce might have found it mortifying. I can't be sure, can't take that chance so out it goes. Think back to your seventh grade science lesson in parallax view: the same event can look completely different depending upon the angle or position of observation, or the distance (physical or emotional!). Ann Landers used to say that 95% of the world's problems would be solved with two words: be kind.

Readers of *Autism Asperger's Digest* first met Bryce as a cover child in 2004, a bright-eyed boy who enjoyed Cub Scouts and Thomas the Tank Engine. No other photos of him have been published until now. What made me decide to make an exception to this privacy policy was this recent portrait taken of him by the same photographer.

I knew the instant the lens clicked this would be one to share; I actually felt faint. Look how far I've come! it declares. No longer a Cub Scout, but a budding filmmaker. Still a Thomas the Tank Engine fan, but with interest in its historical factors; the Thomas toys have all been packed away for the next generation. Bryce exudes the aura of possibility if ever a child did. Possibility, and the celebration of it, is what we should carry with us every day. Not limitation, not fear, not if-only.

Here is where I arrived: I am willing to write about my children without any ego at all. I made plenty of mistakes, put my all into things that didn't work, drowned myself in tsunamis of self-doubt, really got to know what the ceiling above my bed looked like in the dark. Have hated myself more times than I can count—have never, *ever* hated my sons. Stumbled on, even when I couldn't forgive myself. Found that my children were far more resilient and forgiving than I had any right to hope for. All this I have shared, sans sugarcoating, and will continue to share.

What I am not yet willing to write about at length is what the raising of these two children did to my marriage. And yet I am asked: how can you not share this, when it is such an integral part of the story?

You can find any amount of research out there that will tell you the divorce rate for parents of children with autism is 75–80%. How well I can understand that. I am willing to share this about my marriage: my husband and I are still together, over twenty-eight years at this writing. Our vastly different reactions to Bryce's autism did indeed for a time (measured in years) shred the fabric of our marriage to feeble filaments. We stayed together through the downward slide because we never reached a point where we were able to say that the children would be better off with the instability that divorce would create, fracturing the predictability of routines and relationships so critical to them both, shuttling between two homes, enduring the social quagmire of step-parents and step-siblings, the effect the financial strain would have on our ability to seek services for them.

Our thoughts were for our children first. It was plain that they benefited from the constant presence of both father and mother. We stayed together because we each shut out our personal misery. We viewed that misery as temporary, the right attitude, albeit for the wrong reasons ("I'll get out later.").

In the end, we stayed together because our family unit was too precious to destroy and because our history together was too long to throw away. Our strengths and needs still dovetailed; we were still bound by the same values and work ethic and by the things we admired about each other. Our problems were, like those so typical of autism itself, communication malfunctions.

We did finally look for professional help, and found the right person to give it. That I decline to give you the details of what went on in her office is less important than knowing that even when things are bleakest, there's a strong chance you can channel your great love for your child into defying the statistics.

My husband has been unfailingly supportive of my desire to write about our family. He considers it our contribution to making the world better, one reader at a time. He has never once asked me not to write about our marital struggles. Maybe he trusted that I wouldn't; maybe he too thought it was part of the story. But it is my decision alone to write only about the upshot, not the ugly intermediate details. I don't believe that cutting to the chase undercuts the outcome. Both of us had to make changes in how we saw ourselves and each other. I give Mark all the credit in the world for ultimately stepping up to face long-standing fears, irrationalities and non-sequiturs—foul foes that many parents, particularly fathers, are never able to confront.

When you are swimming in a soup of difficulty, it can be a tall order to see past the rim of the bowl. But grab this life preserver: autism awareness and family services are light years beyond where they were just ten years ago, and will only continue to grow. If you reach out for help, you are likely to find it. In a town 1600 miles from home, I met couple who started their own autism social service agency when it became obvious that the local and state government couldn't provide adequately for their daughter with autism and others like her. They repeated to me the counsel they had received along with their daughter's diagnosis: find an institution for her and get yourselves a good marriage counselor. You are going to need both.

Well, the first part is infuriating but the second part is true, isn't it?, I told them. We came within a hair's breadth of not making it.

Who hasn't? the wife replied, her gaze dead-level. *Who hasn't?*

Today, some years later, our family life is not tussle-free. Our children, like all children, are riding the wave of the developmental timeline at the same time we are plunging into serious middle age. Some of the earlier issues of autism have ameliorated and some new ones have arisen. I can tell you that you haven't lived until you've tried living in a household that is a stew of adolescence, autism, ADHD, high school senioritis, and menopause. Oh, the fun we continue to have!

Dish this, with no sugar-coating whatever: autism has brought us moments of great grief and moments of great joy. And I wouldn't trade a moment for any less of either.

A Thing Worth Having

"ANYTHING WORTH HAVING IS WORTH CHEATING FOR," DECLARED W.C. Fields. One need only look to the newspapers to know that too many people agree. Corruption in politics and business is rampant, athletes ingest illicit body-altering substances, students copy essays off the internet and their parents sue the teachers who flunk them for it.

Cheating has always been with us, but it's one aspect of the human condition where some ASD kids, with their sometimes-infuriating black-and-white thinking, are loftily, naturally, above the fray. Back in sixth grade, Bryce brought home a school assignment with two questions to answer: *What is a role model? How should a role model act?* He had very little trouble responding. A role model, he wrote, is someone you admire. His role models: parents, grandparents, uncles, aunts, big brother, cousins and teachers. How should they act? Don't cheat, he wrote. Speak politely and work hard.

We were all thereby put on notice.

I didn't get to know my grandfather, who passed away when I was only four. But I once asked my father what he would tell me about his dad if he could only say one thing. He didn't hesitate with his reply: "He had a great deal of integrity. He never stiffed anyone in his whole life."

Nature or nurture? I think the black-and-white wrongness of cheating may be pronounced in children with autism, but there is also an element of choice in there. It's one of the subjects I muse about when I'm in one of my "Bryce is right and the rest of the world is wrong" moods. It is one of the gifts autism has given our family. Children aren't born knowing how to cheat and wanting to cheat. It is learned in a society that rewards achievement over honesty, winning over trying, the result over the effort. When Connor was in the process of being diagnosed with ADHD, he spent a number of sessions with a psychologist. After one meeting, she had noted a number of atypical things about him, including "he doesn't cheat at games." They had been playing Candy Land™. Well, he had better not, I had replied righteously. What's to cheat at Candy Land? "All kids cheat," was her reply, even though Connor had just disproved the statement. What she meant was, when children are very young, the moral aspect of cheating is absent; they are just playing. But how will they learn that grabbing that extra turn with the dice is not okay, if that gentle adult intervention isn't there from the start? Just playing. Is that like just teasing—which escalates into harassment and bullying?

We should all be a little unsettled with the knowledge that every day in a hundred little ways, we adults look the other way at wrongness and deception and assume it goes over the heads of our children. Then one memorable day we get it in the face, such as the day on which a young Connor came to me with a Curious George book in hand. "The Man in the Yellow Hat is a POACHER. That is another word for ANIMAL SMUGGLER," he declared furiously. Indeed, it's right there in the text—George is happy living in Africa, the Man with the Yellow Hat trapped him with his hat, "popped him into a bag" and took him home. I have to admit I was stunned at how this simple fact had flown under my radar for all the decades of my life. Curious George was never quite the same for me. And that was as it should be, according to Connor, because The Man in the Yellow Hat was a LOSER. "He probably couldn't bag an elephant, so he thought, why not a baby monkey?!"

Bryce seems to have an innate sense of right and wrong, for which I am on-my-knees grateful, as any parent would be. But that ultra-rigid, black-and-white sense of justice did present constant challenges in helping him understand social nuances within the human condition. The older he grew, the more questions he asked about the shades of gray that pervade such things. Is it cheating to knowingly put down a misspelled Scrabble® word if you are pretty sure your opponent won't notice? To watch the movie if you don't finish the book, and answer the book report questions from that? Is it stealing to keep the extra money if a store clerk gives you the wrong change? If you sample the grapes to see if they are sour? And, as he got older, he learned that there are different names for different kinds of cheating, all of them ignoble. Claiming someone's else writing as your own is cheating; it's called plagiarism. Loosening the bolt on your race opponent's bike or car is cheating; it's called sabotage. Lying to gain something that isn't rightfully yours is cheating; it's called "conning." Trick, swindle, deceive, defraud, bamboozle, dupe or bilk—all forms of deception, all soundly rejected by Bryce's unbendable sense of honor.

All of us found our actions under the Brycroscope. When you have a child who craves a concrete explanation for the (abstract) ways of the world, you will meet the challenge of instilling the ability to do the right thing when the right thing is a permutation of a wrong thing—such as a white lie. White lies are rooted in consideration for the feelings of others, something upon which children with ASD may place a lesser value than that of pure fact. Patient explanation over a long period of time may be the only route. We knew we had arrived there on the day I asked Bryce to write a thank-you note for a gift he hadn't particularly liked. "I'll write a white lie," he said. I must have looked surprised because I then received the same sort of patient explanation: "A white lie is when you say something other than the truth in order to make someone feel better. Like saying the dinner was delicious when it wasn't." He had heard this explanation in a movie, and it finally registered.

I have seen that even the youngest children can understand the ignominy of cheating, even in situations that "don't matter." Some years before Bryce was born, my brother's family and mine began vacationing together each summer in a house bordering a golf course at an Oregon resort. The location brought about all kinds of fun. Balls would come flying into the rough—which was also our backyard—and our little boys would run out to snatch them. An ever-lengthening line of golf balls marched down the mantel as the week progressed. Muffled shrieks of glee would vibrate behind the patio door as the wee thieves watched hapless golfers conduct futile searches, sometimes timing them to see how long they'd last before giving up. (Yes, it was stealing, which arguably is as bad as cheating, and this was long before I had a concrete-thinking child with autism to answer to. Standing trial for the crime of sending mixed messages, Judge Bryce presiding, was still in my distant future.) But I told the boys, Aunt Ellie is a big believer in Civil Disobedience. You see, over the years we observed many, many golfers from the deck of that house on the fifth fairway. We didn't start confiscating balls until we had ascertained that an astonishing percentage of those golfers played fast and loose with the rules of sportsmanship. These guys were brazen cheaters. (Yes, guys. We never did see any lady golfers do it.) It was always the same. The furtive glancing around when the ball was located. The tip-toeing back to the green and placing the ball *just so* on the edge. The "Oh! Here it is! Phew—I just lucked out!" The kids, at that time aged between five and eight, never failed to regard this as outrageous behavior.

> *Computer operator:* This machine will now tell us the precise location of the three remaining Gold Tickets.
>
> *Computer read-out:* I won't tell. That would be cheating.
>
> *Willy Wonka and the Chocolate Factory,*
> Warner Brothers, 1971

On a perfect August morning, the boys and I decided to strike a blow for truth-in-golfing. Not content to giggle inside the house any longer, we snuck outside and concealed ourselves behind a very large tree just as the first ball of the day came sailing through the woods. The owner of the ball appeared the predictable number of moments later. He had just taken the requisite look over his shoulder; his fingertips had barely grazed the ball (neatly wedged under a dead log) when I boomed in my best God-sounding baritone: "THAAAAAAT'S CHEEEEEEATING!!!!!"

That poor guy. I don't think he experienced actual heart failure but he definitely suffered some virtual angina, plus whiplash as his head whirled way past 180 degrees searching out his accuser. Ever had that feeling of not really believing something, but at the same time being afraid to not believe it? That guy knew. It was all over his face.

So now you know why one of my all-time favorite comic strips is an old BC panel wherein caveman Peter, inventor of philosophy, is teaching Cute Chick to play golf. Let me see if I understand, she says. The less I hit the ball, the better it is?

That's right, he beams back.

Then why do it at all? she asks.

In the last frame of the strip, it's nighttime. The moon glows above. Peter is hunched over his prehistoric nine-iron, vacant eyes turned heavenward as he ponders, "Why ... do it ... at all?"

So logical. Makes you wonder if there are any golfers with autism. But the same can be said of cheating: why do it at all?

We may call Bryce's black-and-white sense of justice a feature of his autism, but there is another name for it: integrity. "I wish I was like Bryce," one of his third-grade classmates wailed, after some minor behavioral lapse. "Bryce always gets it right." Bryce wouldn't (and shouldn't) necessarily agree, but like his grandfather and great-grandfather father before him, integrity is one of the hallmarks of his life. Autism or inherited? He doesn't have to work at it; it just is. It's a profound legacy, one to which I am still aspiring—neither Dad nor Bryce would have nabbed those golf balls. Dad would have thought that, to a golfer, having us merely sit on the deck, openly but silently witnessing his indignity would be punishment enough. Bryce, had he been around at the time, would have matter-of-factly offered, "You know, you really shouldn't cheat."

Don't cheat, speak politely, work hard. Shall we heed the wisdom of autism? If we can do this, it will be Sam Cooke and not W. C. Fields who prevails: "what a wonderful world this would be."

Pomp and Circumstance

"'Pomp and Circumstance' has become virtually synonymous with school graduation exercises in North America. The reason: the tune manages to sound triumphant, but with an underlying quality of nostalgia, making it perfectly suited to a commencement that marks the beginning of one stage of life, but the end of another."

THE ELGAR SOCIETY AND FOUNDATION

ON MAY 31, 2006 MY OLDEST SON CONNOR WALKED ACROSS A stage and accepted his high school diploma, and a long chapter in my life came to an end.

Three weeks later, Bryce boarded a plane with a group of classmates and teachers and flew 3000 miles across the continent—well out of my reach—and toured New York, Pennsylvania, and Washington DC.

Both of these events were bold leaps toward independence for them, celebrated steps on a continuum that often seemed intent on knocking me backwards.

"Your baby has colic."

"Your son is a textbook case of ADHD."

"Are you familiar with the term autism?"

"It's Crohn's disease."

It seemed like the process of letting go began the minute they were born. Connor slept in a bassinet in our room until he was three weeks old. His perpetual-motion nature was already emerging; he rustled and bustled even in his sleep. We moved him over to his own bedroom, less than ten feet from ours. It seemed like a gulf, and I felt appropriately seasick. I was terrified of SIDS and some nights just stood over his bed watching him breathe. I couldn't know then what a Teflon baby he'd turn out to be; he traveled all the way through childhood with nary an illness or broken bone. Not that the colic and the ADHD weren't challenging enough, but in time I even saw those as but training ground for tangling with the labyrinth of autism.

My mother always said that the most difficult aspect of parenting was knowing when to let go. As a mother myself, I would often fret, *all that and then some!* But once again it was Bryce, with his manner both off-hand and on-target, who helped me crystallize my feelings about letting go.

One otherwise unremarkable day, as we had just put away homework wherein Bryce had written his own Magna Carta, he asked me about a home video taken when he was about eighteen months old. "All of us cousins were playing construction site in the sandbox," he prompted. "Do you remember that?"

Sure I do, I replied.

"I didn't know how to talk then. But I was cute." And then, the unexpected jolt to the heart: "Do you miss those days?"

This is the kind of deeply empathetic question that children with autism are not "supposed" to be able to ask. It actually did take my breath away for a moment. I had to think about it.

I began talking (to myself, or to him?) about how I loved every stage of my children's childhoods. I delighted in my babies learning how to grab Cheerios, stuffing the ball in the Michael Jordan Junior Jammer hoop, faces vanishing as the school bus pulled away, swimming lessons and endless trips to the shoe store as their feet grew like those desiccated sea nymphs dropped in water. How could I not miss my four-year-old Connor wrapping himself around my leg and announcing "Mommy! I wuv you so much, I can't bewieve it!" Or four-year-old Bryce, with his severely limited vocabulary, stepping outside on a particularly foggy, smelly day and recoiling with, "Pyeeuuw! Somebody FARTED!"

Would I miss the late-August arguments: why do you need a $15 Nike™ binder, for heaven's sake? You want corporate advertising plastered across your chest? Either get Warner Bros. and Tommy Hilfiger to pay for it, or pay for it yourself. Connor became a baseball umpire at age thirteen. It only took about three games before he came to me and said, "Now I understand why you don't want to buy me $100 shoes." Those were the kind of moments wherein I knew I had gotten it right.

I faced, gracefully as I could, the end of the bedtime-story era, both grateful and sad because they had reached the day when they could read on their own—and wanted to. And how could I not be proud the year they took over the weekly grocery shopping because they knew the layout of the store, how to read labels, how to choose decent produce and how to use a debit card. The occasional contraband package of Little Debbie's ("Boys, this wasn't on the list!") seemed a small price to pay.

It was impossible not to love every step of their blossoming self-reliance. Can parents of typically-developing children ever appreciate what these increments of independence mean to us special-needs parents? The first time I left Bryce home alone, it was for a whopping seven minutes while I rushed to pick up Connor from a school activity. It seemed like an hour, heart pounding, lip trembling, shallow breathing and all. But soon it became an hour, an afternoon, an evening. A week at Outdoor School. Now a school trip across the continent.

I survived Connor learning to drive. No thunder was ever more deafening that the silence that descended on our driveway as I watched him drive off to work, alone, for the very first time. The fearsome rumble in my head wasn't meteorological; it was my own heart and the boom of the second hand on my watch, ticking off the individual eternities until he reached his destination and checked in safe on arrival. Never was there a moment when I felt more sharply that he had slipped from my control. He could actually be out of the state by the time he checked in safe, and halfway to Canada by the time his work shift ended. He could now be anywhere at any time, and I was going to be at the mercy of his ability to exercise good judgment.

Do you miss those days?

On and on I talked, poor Bryce, by this time trapped in the car listening to waaaay more information than he had bargained for when he asked a simple question.

Do you miss those days?

In the end, the answer was no. Although I loved and treasured those times, all the times that followed were just as wonderful. The "Desiderata" advises us, "Take kindly the counsel of the years, gracefully surrendering the things of youth." It's easier to surrender the things of youth if you are moving ever forward to embrace the gifts of experience and growth.

Letting go is a process, not an event. Connor and I had a ritual every year on the night before his birthday. I would go into his room to say goodnight and lament that "I'm going to miss my six- (seven-, ten-, etc.) year-old!" And he would say, "Don't worry, Mom. You are going to love your (next year's number)-year-old even more!" The night before he turned eighteen was especially hard. I had to go in and say, "I'm going to miss my *child*." And he got to say, "You are going to love the *man* I am going to be."

The next day he went out to buy lottery tickets and register to vote. But he still had a curfew.

Although my children both have special needs that made any kind of complacency impossible, I never allowed their "disorders" to define them, and what they are now is just fine young men. Autism and ADHD will always be part of our lives, but only that—a part. And—lean in closer here—can I tell you that I get just the teeniest amount of perverse pleasure out of hearing parents describe their neurotypical kids as high maintenance—they are too competitive, too perfectionist, too sensitive or insensitive, too hyper, too look-at-me!, unable to entertain themselves, whatever?

"Bloom where you are planted," advises the popular Mary Engelbreit artwork. If I've done my job well, my boys will not only do just that, but will continue to thrive and grow wherever they are transplanted, each to their own unique Field of Dreams.

Leave a Trail

Forward ...

As I write this, I am in residence at Soapstone, a writer's retreat near the Oregon coast. Only two writers are in residence at a time, so the organization tries to match compatible applicants. This week, they hit the bull's-eye. My housemate is Brittney Corrigan, a gifted poet and mother of Elliot, a beautiful three-year-old on the spectrum. Brittney and I became kindred spirits at the first hello (actually, thanks to email, before the first hello). She is writing a chapbook of poems about raising a child on the spectrum. By the fire each night, I listened to her very moving work and knew she had to be a part of this book.

Brittney and her husband Thomas McElroy will welcome a second child this autumn, and she doesn't deny that it's hard to keep the difficult questions at bay. Will this child ...? Bringing a child into the world is an act of courage and faith, and more so when life has already shown you its high curve ball. I lived the uncertainties Brittney is living now while I was expecting Bryce. And even though Bryce did hand me even more challenges than we had already experienced with Connor, through the best and worst of it, I knew that I had the children I was supposed to have and this was the way it was supposed to be. Bryce had drawn the circle around our family that made it complete, and so it will be for Brittney and Thomas and Elliot.

On our last day together at Soapstone, Brittney and I merged our work—she nearer the beginning of her road less traveled and I farther down the road, holding the lantern up. Her poem, "Signs" (in italics) will resonate with every parent who has ever stepped foot on autism's road less traveled. My prose, "Expedition Starts Here," is in response to a question frequently put to me—what is the first advice you would give parents of newly diagnosed children with autism?

Follow us.

SIGNS

My three-year old can name
any sign on the road. He knows
the letters, shapes, symbols, colors.
If we are walking, he likes to touch
the weathered faces, wrap his fingers
around the posts, name and rename

Expedition starts here.

The very first thing you need to know is this: your child is still the same child you fell in love with the moment he/she was placed in your arms for the first time.

Everything you loved about your child before you heard the word "autism" is still there. Everything he/she loves about you is still there. It's just that he/she is going to need you even more than ever.

STOP

Some days, I feel sunk in cement.
I can't move my feet, can't see
past the rain in my eyes. The world
approaches, stares, leaves us behind.
We perseverate together—he recites
the letters again and again.
S. T. O. P. No instructions
for which way to turn.

Face forward.

You can do this.

When you signed on to become a parent, you did so because you thought you were up to the task. It's okay to admit that having a child with extraordinary needs may not have entered your thoughts. Now faced with something other than a "regular" kid, you may feel that you are in over your head.

You are definitely swimming in deeper waters, but being in over your head doesn't mean doing it in cement boots. With the right training and gear, many people swim for miles in water over their heads. I can still see myself as a child, with my swim teacher walking our class to the deep end of the pool for the first time. "There is nothing different about the water in this end of the pool," he said. "It's not any wetter, it's not any bluer, it's not any colder. The only difference is that bottom is farther down." He pointed out that since we would be swimming on the surface of the water, it really didn't matter how far down the bottom was.

Then—the clever devil—he told us that human bodies have buoyancy and that we couldn't sink to the bottom unless we really tried. You can guess where this went. After a few sprints across the pool to prove that we could in fact survive being in over our heads, we took to jumping off the diving board with enough velocity to touch bottom, twelve feet down. Knowing exactly how far down the bottom was only increased our confidence.

Sometimes we forgot to exhale on the way down, getting a searing rush of chlorinated water up the snout. Little injuries and indignities do occur when you are in over your head, but they need not hold you down and under.

Bottom line: being in over your head is not synonymous with drowning, or even flailing. You are buoyant.

Your child loves you and needs you. You can do this.

YIELD

The road moves in to meet us. Hands
on the wheel, I resist taking my turn.
I'm afraid if we merge, we'll be stuck
in this traffic forever. We'll never
get home. Someone honks. I inch forward,
check the blind spots, shift gears.

For the duration of the trip …

Time is on your side.

Wanting to know everything there is to know about autism as soon as the diagnosis comes down is the typical and understandable reaction of many parents. But it is possible to overwhelm yourself with information (some of it contradictory). Coming out of the gate confused and conflicted is not the way you want to begin your journey. Marathons require stamina in addition to speed.

Rather, start by knowing that you have lots of time guide your child to adulthood—years and years. It will be a process, not an event, and progress *will* come. Explore resources and opportunities as they present themselves, knowing that your child's needs will grow and change as he travels the developmental timeline. Yours will too—

you are also on a developmental journey, and you too have your own unique spot on the autism spectrum. Growing along with you, on a daily basis, are knowledge and insights in medical science and education. In the face of such exponentially increasing opportunity, no previous generation has ever had more reason to be optimistic about the future of our children with autism.

Your child loves you and needs you. You can do this. Time is on your side.

NO U-TURN

We wouldn't go back even if we could. We have navigated dodgy side streets, gotten lost, asked for directions. Used up a profusion of fuel. We've sat in noisy intersections, wound down quiet roads. He points ahead. This way.

Ask for directions.

Listen to your inner voice.

It's true. You are the foremost authority on your child. No one knows her better or loves her more. But being the foremost authority doesn't equate to being a know-it-all. When you freely trust your instinct, that little voice will frequently tell you to seek more information, look for a different solution, find other services, other professionals, even other friends. It *is* important to listen to practitioners, teachers and other parents, but their experiences, however successful for them, are not mandatory for your child. Listen to your inner voice if it tells you that a particular program, diet, school or treatments isn't right for your child.

The "It" program is never the only one out there. Keep looking.

Your child loves you and needs you. You can do this. Time is on your side. Listen to your inner voice.

ONE WAY

Forget about the map. We memorized
its lines, then left it at the rest stop
three states back. This is only one direction,
one arrow, and he wants to see
them all. Left turn, right turn, two-way
traffic, curve. We might go around the block.
We might drive for miles and miles.

Level pavement ...

Strike a balance.

Buy into the idea of balance before you've allowed your child's autism to envelop you. Actually, there are several delicate balances we need to strike, so when you start to feel like a juggler, remember that jugglers are cool and, with practice, they get the routine down and seldom drop the ball.

For your child. Strive always to balance the demands of autism with typical child development that will be happening right alongside. Your child is not a packet of symptoms or malfunctioning parts. Those typical-development needs are no less essential.

For your family. Your child with autism will place extraordinary requirements on you, but do not let his needs blockade him from the rest of the family and community. Don't focus your energy on him in a manner that suggests that other members of the family are less important. Treat him as the whole person he is, a full-fledged member of your family, with age-appropriate responsibilities to the other members. Neglecting the needs of siblings who are also works-in-progress, not allowing time for extended family and friends, letting professional appointments and services completely dictate family life—all of these send a message to the child that she is the center of a universe around which everyone else revolves. It's not a message she can take into productive, independent adulthood.

For yourself. Nurture all facets of yourself, not just your parent persona. Letting your child see you as a versatile adult who is involved in the extended family and community, pursues hobbies, enjoys friendships, takes care of her own health, allows herself fun and respite—this sets the best kind of whole-person example for your child.

On some days, all this balancing may seem close to impossible. Nothing is more poignant than the letters I get from moms who must write words like these: "My son was diagnosed at age three-and-a-half. He has two brothers who love him no matter what, but sometimes they ask me, 'Do I have to have autism for you to love me?' I cry and say no, of course not, it's just that Jonathan needs Mommy's attention a little more than you guys."

Other days, the stars will line up and you will get it just right. On those days, you will experience the joy of what is possible and the confidence of knowing the process is working.

Your child loves you and needs you. You can do this. Time is on your side. Listen to your inner voice. Strike a balance.

BUMPS

We spend a lot of time with this sign.
It's one of his favorites—we see
it on our daily walk. We know
its shape, its angles, its warning face. But
the road between us and the playground
is in constant flux. Broken glass, a new
flower, bees. And always, he must
touch this sign before we can go home.

Junction ...

You will always have choices.

Sometimes you will not like the choices, and sometimes the choices will be downright bad. But there are always choices, and learning to recognize the full range of choices available in any situation will help you immeasurably in making the right ones (even from a slate of lousy choices) and feeling confident in your ability to make those choices. Become aware that your daily life is a continuum of choices that you make minute by minute—what to wear, where to go, when to go, how to get there, what goes into your mouth, what comes out of your mouth, how to question your boss, how to answer your children ... and on and on. It's a gift not only to have so many choices, but to have the ability to choose.

The ability to choose gives you ultimate control over your life. And because you will always have both the choices and the ability to choose, the way things are today does not have to be the way things are tomorrow.

We've all heard the aphorism that "autism happens to the whole family." While it is certainly true that the needs of the child with autism can affect the whole family, the only one it's really happening to is the child. This is the rare instance in which someone had no choice in the matter, and that someone is your child. The rest of the family has myriad choices in how they choose to deal with it or not deal with it, and therein lies the inescapable responsibility, and the inescapable opportunity:

The right choice for your child will almost always be the right choice for you.

CONSTRUCTION AHEAD

We might be here awhile. Expect delays.
Or maybe it's Sunday and the workers
have the day off, the road signs are pushed

to the side. But we're curious. What
are they building? Does it have scaffolding,
are they tearing up the street? When
we round the next corner, will there be
a road block, a detour, a flagger waving
us through? I look back at him.
Green light. Go.

Ready. Set. *Green light. Go.*

Along this road less traveled, you will always have choices. Strike a balance. Listen to your inner voice. Time is on your side. Your child loves you and needs you.

You can do this.

Ellen Notbohm
April 12, 2007
Soapstone writing retreat for women
near Nehalem, Oregon

About the Author

BOOK AUTHOR, COLUMNIST AND MOTHER OF SONS WITH AUTISM AND ADHD, Ellen Notbohm's writings on autism and general interest subjects have been published on every continent (except Antarctica—yet). Her previous books, *Ten Things Every Child with Autism Wishes You Knew* and *Ten Things your Student with Autism Wishes You Knew* are both ForeWord Book of the Year finalists and iParenting Media Award recipients. A regular columnist for *Autism Asperger's Digest* magazine and *Children's Voice,* she also co-authored with Veronica Zysk *1001 Great Ideas for Teaching and Raising Children with Autism Spectrum Disorders,* a Learning Magazine 2006 Teacher's Choice Award winner.

Beyond autism, she is a frequent contributor to Ancestry magazine, has published political commentary in the Chicago Tribune and other newspapers around the US, and writes for numerous regional and national magazines on a range of subjects.

Ellen welcomes reader feedback and newsletter signs-ups through her website at *www.ellennotbohm.com.*